KNOWING GOD
IN THE LAST DAYS

KNOWING GOD
IN THE LAST DAYS

COMMENTARY ON 2 PETER

Mark H. Hoeksema

REFORMED
FREE PUBLISHING
ASSOCIATION
Jenison, Michigan

Reformed Free Publishing Association
1894 Georgetown Center Drive
Jenison, Michigan 49428
rfpa.org
mail@rfpa.org
616-457-5970

Cover design by Erika Kiel
Interior design and typesetting by Katherine Lloyd, the DESK

ISBN 978-1-944555-22-1
Ebook 978-1-944555-23-8
LCCN 2017946331

To the past and present staff of
the Reformed Free Publishing Association
which has provided many insights
and much enouragement

CONTENTS

CHAPTER TWO • 41

CHAPTER THREE • 67

FOREWORD

This commentary on 2 Peter is a valuable resource for the church of Christ.

Its value lies in its brevity. There is certainly a place in the lives of God's people for longer and deeper commentaries on each book of the Bible, and many have been written. Such is not this volume. Instead, it is concise and to the point, briefly explaining 2 Peter verse by verse. The commentary will be excellent for a quick read to grasp the book as a whole in its general themes, for a needed reference to understand a particular section, for the family to read aloud around the dinner table for family worship, or for believers in a Bible study to generate thoughts and discussions on this portion of God's word.

The commentary's value lies in its clarity. The author's style is refreshing. As a capable editor of many other works, the author understands well how to wield the English language effectively, which comes through clearly in this work.

The commentary's value also lies in its perspective. It is written from the viewpoint of the Reformed faith, and shows conviction of the doctrines of grace as they are set forth in the three forms of unity. Writing from this perspective, the author honors God as the sovereign creator and redeemer of his people through the person and work of the Lord Jesus Christ.

More could be said to explain the good resource that this commentary is for the church today. I let the work speak for itself, and I pray that the Spirit of Jesus Christ will use this work to guide his saints to a better understanding of the truth.

—Rev. Nathan Decker

INTRODUCTION

U ntil recently commentators have largely ignored the second general epistle of Peter. The reason is difficult to determine. Perhaps this has to do with its brevity or with its content, or with both. Perhaps this is because the second epistle of Peter has stood in the shadow of the first epistle of Peter. But the fact is indisputable.

Of late, however, there has been a resurgence of interest in 2 Peter. A number of commentators have recently taken up the pen in explanation of the epistle.

Authorship and Canonicity

This renewal of interest has been fraught with controversy. To ignore this fact is to do injustice to the scriptures. Beginning already with the early church and continuing until the present, there has been disagreement regarding two major issues. The first concerns the identity of the human writer of the epistle; some in the history of the church have denied that Peter is the writer. The second concerns its canonicity.

The two are intertwined. Either Peter is the human writer of the epistle, or he is not. If he is, his epistle belongs to the canon of scripture because the Holy Spirit inspired him. If he is not, his epistle does not belong to the canon but is a forgery and a fake. Conversely, if the book, according to the judgment of the church,

1

is canonical, Peter must be the human writer. If the epistle is not canonical, Peter cannot be the writer.

Although the arguments pro and con are sketchy, they date to the first three centuries, continue through the time of the Reformation, and intensify in the twentieth century. Most of the argumentation, while scholarly, is technical and arcane and therefore not helpful to God's people.

While many commentators with various degrees of complexity and clarity address these issues, Simon Kistemaker is perhaps the clearest. In the introduction to his commentary, he devotes nineteen pages to the issues and disagreements. In so doing he draws correct conclusions based on the evidence.[1]

Much of modern scholarship, which often denies that Peter is the human writer, thus denying the canonicity of 2 Peter, smacks of higher criticism and must be rejected. The correct view is that the apostle Peter is the human writer of this epistle and that it therefore is canonical.

This view is confirmed by Peter himself in 1:13–15, where he asserts that he wrote the epistle:

13. Yea, I think it meet, as long as I am in this tabernacle, to stir you up by putting you in remembrance;
14. Knowing that shortly I must put off this my tabernacle, even as our Lord Jesus Christ hath shewed me.
15. Moreover I will endeavour that ye may be able after my decease to have these things always in remembrance.

Reformed—and all Bible-believing—Christians assert that because scripture interprets itself, Peter's words are to be accepted as truth. Peter speaks in verse 15 of "these things," a clear reference

---

1 Simon J. Kistemaker, *New Testament Commentary* (Grand Rapids, MI: Baker Book House, 1987), 5–24.

to what he intends to teach the church and what the church must remember after his death. Besides, and most significantly, in 1:1 Peter identifies himself as an apostle, which means that he is the divinely inspired writer of the epistle who writes as the authoritative representative of Christ.

Date

The date of this epistle cannot be ascertained precisely. Estimates vary widely, depending on one's view of the authorship and canonicity of the letter. Those who deny that Peter wrote the book and reject the book's canonicity assign to it a second-century date, but they are wrong.

Peter himself in 1:13–14 indicates that he writes this letter shortly before his imminent demise. The early church historian Eusebius places the date of Peter's death during Nero's persecution of the church during AD 64–68.

Further, Peter was acquainted with Paul's writings (3:15–16). Therefore this epistle could not have been one of the earliest New Testament writings.

Taking into account these facts, it is likely that Peter wrote this epistle shortly before AD 68.

Recipients

In 2 Peter the apostle does not state directly to whom he writes. In 1:1 he identifies them only as those who "have obtained like precious faith with us through the righteousness of God." In contrast, the apostle in 1 Peter identifies his readers as those who live in Pontus, Galatia, Cappadocia, Asia, and Bithynia.

Yet there is a definite connection between the two epistles. This link is evident from 2 Peter 3:1, where the apostle describes this letter as his second epistle, a clear reference to 1 Peter. The recipients of 2 Peter, then, are the same saints of Asia Minor to whom he wrote 1 Peter.

As in 1 Peter, he writes to the churches in general, including both Jewish and Gentile Christians. Nothing suggests that he addresses a particular group or that he deals with a problem specific to any situation, such as a doctrinal error or a practical issue.

Theme and Purpose

The theme of 2 Peter is the knowledge of God. Peter uses the word *knowledge* and its related forms no fewer than eleven times in this brief epistle. In 1:2–3, 5–6, 8; 2:20; 3:18 he uses the term *knowledge*. In 1:20; 2:9; 3:3, 17 he uses various verb forms of the word.

The epistle, although short, contains a wealth of instruction for the church, which explains why its theme is the true knowledge of God. This theme the apostle develops and applies to his readers. In chapter 1 he exhorts the Christians to grow in the knowledge of God and of Christ as revealed in the word of prophecy given through the apostles. Having received the promises, they are to add to their faith various spiritual virtues, including knowledge. In chapter 2 the apostle warns against false teachers, whom believers can recognize and reject only if they have the true knowledge of God. In chapter 3 Peter applies true knowledge to the end times and describes appropriate Christian behavior in light of the final judgment and the renewal of all things.

The purpose of the epistle is to teach the knowledge of God and of Christ. It is impossible to know God without knowing Jesus as his Son. The purpose is to strengthen Christians in true knowledge and faith in opposition to false teachers, about whom Peter has much to say, especially in chapter 2. It is further the purpose to give instruction concerning the end times in contrast to those who deny Christ's second coming and the final judgment. Christians must live as those who are in the end times.

Character

Peter's letter is not easy to interpret because he often uses words found nowhere else in scripture. In chapter 3 alone he does this six times. One of the principles of understanding the Bible is that scripture interprets scripture, which sometimes makes his meaning difficult to discern because he does not use identical or even comparative terms that are used elsewhere in scripture. In addition, in keeping with his character, Peter is often blunt, very graphic, and sometimes almost abusive in his language. He is definitely not politically correct.

Division

I have divided the content of this epistle into verses and sections for purposes of organization and clarity. Although these divisions are helpful, they are somewhat artificial. Peter did not write an outline but a personal letter to the church of his day, and this must always be kept in mind. His letter is a unity, and its continuity must be recognized.

Perspective

This hardly needs to be said, but my perspective as a Reformed Christian is that 2 Peter is the inspired and infallible word of God and must be explained as such. In the interpretation of this epistle I also subscribe to the doctrines taught in the three forms of unity—the Belgic Confession, the Heidelberg Catechism, and the Canons of Dordrecht.

CHAPTER ONE

Greeting: 1:1–2

1. Simon Peter, a servant and an apostle of Jesus Christ, to them that have obtained like precious faith with us through the righteousness of God and our Saviour Jesus Christ:
2. Grace and peace be multiplied unto you through the knowledge of God, and of Jesus our Lord.

Peter begins his letter to the churches by identifying himself as Simon Peter. More correctly, he gives his name as Simeon, the Jewish form of Simon. This name is usually used in the New Testament and in Hebrew is a form of Samuel, which means God has heard. Peter's reason for using his given name, Simeon, is to express his unity with his Jewish readers, who undoubtedly knew its meaning.

The apostle also identifies himself as Peter, the name that Jesus gave him (Matt. 16:18). Christ gave him the name *Petros* (*Rock* in Greek), which in the Aramaic is Cephas, a form infrequently used in scripture. That Peter is the rock on which Christ will build his church may not be misinterpreted, as does the Roman Catholic Church, as referring to Peter personally, from which Rome deduces that Peter was the first pope. Rather, Peter is the rock on which the church is built from the viewpoint of his confession that Jesus is the

Christ, the Son of the living God (Matt. 16:16–18). By frequently using these twin appellations, as he does here, the apostle acknowledges that he is both Simon and Peter.

The apostle is the Jewish fisherman whom the Lord called to follow him as his disciple. He is Simon according to his weak and often sinful nature. He belongs to the old covenant, and he frequently does not understand the meaning and nature of Jesus' kingdom. Being of a somewhat brash and hasty nature, he sometimes stumbles and falls in his pilgrim journey of faith, notably when he denied the Lord.

Yet Peter is also *Petros*, his distinctively Christian name. As the spokesman for the other disciples, he confessed that Jesus is the Messiah. Being enlightened by the outpouring of the Holy Spirit, he preached his famous Pentecost sermon. As the rock he understands that the gospel of Christ must go to Jew and Gentile alike, and to that church he writes his epistles.

Peter, now an old man, knows himself. He knows that he is both Simeon and *Petros*, and as such he addresses his letter to the churches. Undoubtedly the church of his day knew exactly what he meant when he used this double identification.

Peter goes on to describe himself in two more related ways. He calls himself a servant and an apostle. The word rendered as "servant" in the King James Version is correctly translated as "slave." There is a difference. A servant is someone who voluntarily serves another. He is hired to perform a service, usually by means of a contract or other agreement, and he is paid for services rendered. A simple example makes this clear. If I hire someone to mow my lawn, we sign a contract that spells out the duties to be performed and the amount of money to be paid for the service. However, the relationship between the customer and the service company is voluntary. The lawn maintenance company is not the slave of the customer. Either party can terminate the relationship at will. Such is the idea of servanthood.

Slavery, however, is different. It carries with it not the idea of a relationship between equals, but the idea of ownership: one person owns another. Their relationship has an involuntary aspect. Unlike a servant, a slave mows his owner's grass whether or not he wants to do so, and he is not paid to do it. He cannot terminate a contract and walk away, but he is bound in servitude to his master. Never mind that in Peter's day slaves were frequently viewed as being almost members of the families of those whom they served. They belonged to their owners.

Peter uses the idea of slavery, so common in the Roman world, to describe himself. He is a slave of Jesus Christ. From a spiritual viewpoint he belongs to Jesus. Christ owns him, body and soul. Jesus has bought him by means of his atoning death. Christ has regenerated him, called him, justified him, and sanctified him. Thus the apostle belongs to him. The relationship between Christ and Peter is not voluntary or contractual, but that of ownership. Because Christ has redeemed him, Peter in his whole being and life belongs to Christ, along with his readers, who are also slaves of Christ. By thus describing himself, Peter puts himself on the same plane as his readers: together they willingly and lovingly belong to Christ, their lord and master.

Peter also describes himself as "an apostle." The word is the noun form of a verb that means to send or to commission, which implies that there is one who commissions or sends, in this instance, Christ, who chooses to send his gospel by means of his emissaries. Peter does not write his own ideas and words, but he speaks only those given to him by Christ through the inspiration of the Holy Spirit. His teachings therefore are authoritative because he belongs to Jesus Christ, who sent him as an apostle to preach and teach the gospel.

In his capacity both as a slave and as an apostle, Peter addresses those who "have obtained like precious faith with us."

Faith in scripture can have two meanings. Sometimes it is used objectively, so that it refers to the content of faith. It is what we believe, the doctrines of the Christian faith. Sometimes faith is used subjectively, so that it refers to the act of believing, the trust that believers place in God. There is no dichotomy between objective and subjective faith, although there is a distinction. The two senses are like the two sides of a coin: related but not separated.

Commentators disagree regarding the use of the term here, but the evidence points to the subjective meaning of faith.

This faith is described as "like precious…with us." "Like precious" literally means "of like value or significance," and thus precious. The idea of a precious and similar faith, Peter says, is shared "with us." Peter refers to himself and the other apostles, all of whom shared a personal trust in Christ. Peter uses the pronoun "us" to show that the faith of his readers is the same as that of the apostles. By so doing he unites himself with his readers.

Peter goes on to say that he and his readers have obtained this like precious faith "through the righteousness of God and our Saviour Jesus Christ." More correctly the text reads "in" the righteousness of God and our Saviour Jesus Christ, that is, in the sphere of or in connection with this righteousness. The meaning is that faith is always connected with righteousness. It is only in the sphere of righteousness that faith is possible and is our possession.

Righteousness in scripture has more than one meaning. It can refer to the divine attribute (Ps. 145:17; Rom. 3:26; 1 John 2:29), in which case it means that all of God's willing and acting are in perfect harmony with his holiness. It can also mean justification, the imputed righteousness accomplished through the atoning death of Christ, so that God's elect people are judged to be in harmony with the holiness of God (Rom. 4:22–25). It can also refer to sanctification, by which God delivers his people from the dominion of sin and enables them to walk in holiness (Matt. 5:6; Rom. 6:18). These three ideas may be distinguished but not separated.

There is a difference among commentators as to which aspect of righteousness is meant here. It seems that the emphasis falls on the righteousness of God as his divine virtue. Therefore, the term "God" in this instance refers to the triune God as he is revealed in Jesus Christ. Peter connects faith with righteousness, so that the meaning is that God imparts this righteousness to those who have been given faith, that is, to those who believe.

God is our savior. Peter calls God "our Saviour Jesus Christ." He is Jesus, Jehovah salvation. He is Christ, the promised Messiah. Revealed as Jesus Christ, savior from sin, God is in harmony with his perfect righteousness. That righteousness is imputed to his elect through the death of Christ, so that they are justified, and is then realized in the sanctification of God's people. Thus those who have faith believe in God our savior as he is revealed in Jesus Christ.

The words *grace and peace* are often used by the apostles as their salutation to the churches (Rom. 1:7; 1 Cor. 1:3; 2 Cor. 1:2), and this is no exception. *Grace* in scripture has many nuances and applications, but its basic meaning is God's favor. Grace is that which affords joy, pleasure, and delight. It is charm and loveliness, the opposite of disfavor, displeasure, and wrath. Peace is negatively the absence of war and conflict; positively, it is harmony, tranquility, and concord.

Peter says, "Grace and peace be multiplied unto you." He uses a verb form that expresses a wish: he wishes that grace and peace will be increased to his readers. Peter, however, does not express this wish from a purely personal and human viewpoint. If this were the case, his wish would carry with it no weight or power, but would be no more significant than anyone else's wish.

Instead, Peter writes as an apostle, as he asserts in verse 1. He writes authoritatively, as an official representative of God and of Christ. Therefore, his wish actually conveys grace and peace to the church. This idea is reinforced by the passive voice of the verb: be multiplied. This expression implies an agent—someone who does the increasing or multiplying. That someone is God.

When we put these ideas together, the meaning is that God through the apostle conveys his grace and peace to his people.

This increase of grace and peace is "in [not through] the knowledge of God, and of Jesus our Lord." The knowledge of which Peter writes is not a general or secular knowledge. Rather, the word is used in the New Testament and here to indicate ethical and divine knowledge. More specifically, it refers to precise and correct knowledge. This implies that God is the originator and author of this knowledge. Grace and peace are conditioned by true knowledge.

Surely the knowledge of which Peter speaks is an intellectual knowledge. From scripture we know the truths of Jesus' incarnation, his life and ministry, his suffering and death, his resurrection and ascension, and his promised return. But this knowledge is also spiritual and experiential. It is not sufficient to know the hard, cold facts of the life and death of the Lord. Rather, the knowledge of which Peter speaks applies to God's elect people, who are the beneficiaries of the life, death, and resurrection of Christ.

This is why Peter characterizes this knowledge as "of God, and of Jesus our Lord." This knowledge is God's; he is its author. This knowledge is that of Jesus, Jehovah salvation, and of our lord, our ruler and king. What a great and glorious grace and peace are ours in the knowledge of God through Jesus Christ!

Great and Precious Promises: 1:3–4

3. According as his divine power hath given unto us all things that pertain unto life and godliness, through the knowledge of him that hath called us to glory and virtue:
4. Whereby are given unto us exceeding great and precious promises: that by these ye might be partakers of the divine nature, having escaped the corruption that is in the world through lust.

Commentators are divided as to whether or not verses 3 and 4 are connected with verses 1 and 2. The textual evidence and the grammar, as well as the thought and meaning, indicate that there is a connection between these verses. Peter expresses this relation by "according as," which has the sense of "because." The connection is that grace and peace (v. 2) are multiplied in accordance with or because of God's divine power. This means that God's power through Christ is effectual. Grace and peace are the believers' possession because of God's power.

There is also a difference of opinion as to whether or not the words "his" and "him" in verse 3 refer to God or to Jesus. Does "his divine power" refer to God or to Christ? Does "the knowledge of him" refer to God or to Christ? The weight of the evidence seems to be on Christ, since these pronouns have "Jesus our Lord" as their antecedent. But which option is correct does not matter greatly, since both God and Jesus Christ are mentioned in verse 2.

The divine power of verse 3 is God's, as is God's knowledge. God's is all divine power and all knowledge, but his power and knowledge are always through Jesus Christ. Christ is the revelation of God, and he reveals his power and knowledge only through

Christ. This is true because Christ is God, the second person of the Trinity according to his divine nature. Therefore, the reference of the pronouns makes little difference.

The word Peter uses to describe God's power means strength or ability. From this word we obtain the English word *dynamite*. The word is descriptive. If one wishes to mine stone from a quarry, he drills a hole in the rock, inserts a stick of dynamite, lights its fuse, and as the result of the powerful explosion that ensues, obtains the loose stone he desires. The point is that the dynamite by its power accomplishes its purpose.

Peter uses this descriptive term in a spiritual sense. He refers to the divine power whereby God accomplishes all his good pleasure. By his power he has created all things and continues to uphold them by the strength of his providence. By that same power God accomplishes salvation. By the Spirit he regenerates his elect. By the power of his word he calls sinners from the darkness of sin into the light of his salvation. By the gift of his Son he justifies his chosen ones, and by the power of his Holy Spirit he sanctifies them, changing sinners into saints. Finally, by his power he defeats and destroys the kingdom of darkness and establishes the everlasting kingdom of his Son, of which his people are the heirs.

That power of God has given us all things. "All things" are further described as "life and godliness." The idea is that God's divine power has given and continues to give us everything necessary for life and godliness.

Peter uses a common New Testament word when he speaks of life. *Life* can mean physical existence, our life on this earth, beginning with birth and ending with death. Often it also refers to spiritual life, the new life of regeneration and sanctification. Above all, the reference is to eternal life, as it is here. This life is the blessedness of eternal, unending glory in the new heavens and new earth, which we possess now in principle through the indwelling of the Holy Spirit, and which will be ours perfectly and completely in the world to come.

Peter goes on to say that by God's power he gives us "godliness," which means reverence and respect. It is piety, not in the sense of a mystical spirituality, but in the sense of a deep respect for who God is and therefore a reverence toward him as the sovereign God in comparison with us as mere creatures. Godliness is the fear of the Lord, according to which we submit to him and walk in his ways. The manifestation of the principle of eternal life that dwells in us is our respect and reverence toward God. Such is the connection between life and godliness.

This giving to us all things pertaining to life and godliness is "through the knowledge of him that hath called us to glory and virtue."

The knowledge of which Peter writes is the same knowledge of which he writes in verse 2, that is, a spiritual and experiential knowledge of God in Christ. God gives us all the blessings of salvation through, or by means of, this knowledge. We must know God in order to understand and experience life and godliness. Thus life and godliness are through knowledge. This makes sense: it is impossible to understand life and godliness without knowing what they are.

This is reinforced by "him that hath called us." The one who has called us is God. The calling of which Peter speaks here is not the preaching of the gospel as it is proclaimed by the church. Rather, it refers to the work of God's grace by which he saves his elect people by calling them from darkness to light and from death to life. It is the saving, effectual calling. This calling is connected with the knowledge of God in that without his saving calling we cannot know God experientially.

God has called us to glory and virtue. God's calling is the demonstration of his glory and virtue. Glory and virtue are the goal of God's calling: to glory and virtue he has called us. More precisely, by the great gift of life and holiness bestowed on us, God has made us partakers of his own glory and virtue.

God's glory is the manifestation of all of his attributes. The example of the sun makes this idea clear. The light of the sun is the glory of the sun, and the glory of the sun is the radiation of its light. So it is with God's glory. God has many attributes: omnipotence, omniscience, omnipresence, immutability, sovereignty, holiness, wisdom, love, grace, mercy, longsuffering, and righteousness. His glory is the radiation or manifestation of his divine being in such a way that man knows and can understand who and what God is. God's glory, then, is the ultimate goal or end of all things. God must be revealed in all his perfections, and that revelation is his glory.

God's glory is also his virtue. Glory and virtue are not exactly synonymous, but they are closely related. Virtue means excellence or eminent property or quality. The emphasis of virtue falls on God's goodness or holiness and is thus more specific than his glory. Glory is the more general idea, while virtue or goodness is more specific. Nevertheless, God's virtue is his glory, and his glory is his goodness. To participate in his glory and virtue God has called us.

Peter connects verse 3 to verse 4 by "whereby," that is, "through which," in the plural. He refers to "all things that pertain unto life and godliness." Through the things that have been given to us by God's power, the things that pertain to life and godliness, we have received exceeding great and precious promises.

The apostle uses the word "promises" in the plural. Scripture uses the term in both the singular and the plural. When the word is singular, as it often is, it refers to the oneness or unity of the promise. As God is one, as Christ is one, as the church is one, as salvation is one, so the promise is one. The reason for the singular form is that the promise is always and essentially Christ, whether in the Old or in the New Testament, and thus one.

The use of both singular and plural forms can be understood from the example of the rainbow. As a single beam of white light is refracted into the seven colors of a rainbow, so the one promise is distinguished into the many riches of many promises. All the blessings of salvation—the forgiveness of sins, adoption unto children, righteousness, faith, hope, the new heavens and new earth—are all so many promises that God gives to his church through the Spirit of Christ.

These promises are described as "exceeding great and precious." The word translated as "exceeding great" is a superlative adjective meaning most great. From this word we derive the English prefix *mega*, meaning million, so that we may speak of mega promises. They are mega because they are the promises of the mega God, the sovereign of the universe, through whom his people enjoy mega salvation.

The promises of God are also described as "precious," that is, costly and of great price. The word immediately makes us think of diamonds or other precious gems that are worth large sums of money. Such are the promises of God. They are of great value, greater than anything else in this world, and are therefore to be treasured. They are so precious that their fulfillment cost God his only begotten Son.

Peter says that we are given these great and precious promises with the purpose, or the result, that we may be partakers of the divine nature. This is a startling statement and one that is difficult to explain. We, mere specks of dust, less than nothing, are given the promises with the purpose of becoming partakers of the divine? What can this mean?

Negatively, this clause cannot mean that somehow we become divine, as the Buddhist and Hindu religions teach. Nor can this mean what the Greek philosophers of Peter's day taught, which was that man, living in the corrupt world of physical pleasure, needed to become like the pantheon of the gods in order to become like the divine nature. Peter here uses the terminology of Greek humanistic philosophy, but he borrows it for use in a Christian context when he speaks of being partakers of the divine nature. Without doubt his readers understood his point

Positively, in order to understand what Peter says, we must draw a careful distinction between God's being, or essence, and his nature. God's being is his essence, according to which he is God in contrast to us, who are creatures made by him. God is God. Man is creature. God's divine nature, in contrast, refers to his ethical or communicable attributes. The two may not be confused. We as creatures cannot ever be partakers of God's being. Nevertheless, we can and do share, in a creaturely way, his ethical attributes in the light of God's promises.

Thus we are partakers not of his being or essence, but of his divine nature. Spiritually and ethically we are like God. We are partakers of the image of God: true knowledge, righteousness, and holiness. We know God as he has revealed himself to us. We are righteous, albeit in principle, as he is perfectly righteous. We are holy as he is holy, again in principle. Having been begotten again, not of corruptible seed but of incorruptible, through the word of God that lives and abides forever, we enjoy fellowship with him. The restoration of the image of God in us does not deify us, but it does make us partakers of God's perfect nature. We anticipate that we, as partakers of the divine nature, ultimately will inherit the kingdom of God, in which we will perfectly participate in his perfect nature.

Peter says that we are partakers of the divine nature, "having escaped the corruption that is in the world through lust." The two are direct opposites: we become partakers of the divine nature by escaping the corruption in the world. They are mutually exclusive and incapable of compromise.

Peter speaks of corruption, that which rots and perishes. We are reminded of Jesus' words in Matthew 6:19: "Lay not up for yourselves treasures upon earth, where moth and rust doth corrupt, and where thieves break through and steal." Peter refers to corruption in the ethical sense of moral decay. He uses this descriptive word for sin from the viewpoint of its manifestation: it is not sin *per se*, but it is the corruption and rottenness of sin that ends in perdition.

This corruption is described as being "in the world." *World* can have different meanings in scripture, depending on the context in which it is used, but here it means the world of wicked men, those who are deliberately alienated from God and who are hostile to the cause of Christ. It is the world in which the church must live and develop in fellowship with the divine nature. World in this sense and church are therefore inimical. This corruption is evident in the world today. We need to think only of the slaughter of many thousands of unborn infants by means of the unspeakable evil of legalized abortion, to say nothing of the legalization and promotion of so-called same-sex or homosexual marriage, the sin for which God destroyed Sodom and Gomorrah.

We have escaped the corruption that is in the world "through lust." We immediately think of lust in a sexual sense, but this is not entirely correct. "Lust," as Peter uses the term, means all carnal and earthly desires that are forbidden by God without limitation or restriction. Scripture describes this as the lust of the flesh, the lust of the eyes, and the pride of life (1 John 2:16). Lust or desire is in itself not wrong as long as such desire is in harmony with the divine nature: we may and should covet to be like all of God's wonderful perfections. But when desire becomes a carnal desire of any sort, whether sexual lust, a lust for money, fame, power, or any other inappropriate lust, it is wrong.

Lust and corruption are related. Corruption is the manifestation of lust: lust brings forth corruption. Corruption is sin against both tables of the law of God: it is enmity against God and hatred against the neighbor. It reveals itself in all spheres and aspects of man's life—corruption of the individual, corruption in society, and corruption in the nations.

From this corruption through lust we have escaped, says Peter. His use of the word "escaped" implies that we were previously in bondage. Indeed, we were enslaved by the rottenness and corruption of the world, imprisoned by the power of lust. But empowered by God's grace given to us by the Holy Spirit, we have in principle broken the bonds of sin and are now free to serve our saving God through Christ.

A Chain of Virtues: 1:5–7

5. And beside this, giving all diligence, add to your faith virtue; and to virtue knowledge;
6. And to knowledge temperance; and to temperance patience; and to patience godliness;
7. And to godliness brotherly kindness; and to brotherly kindness charity.

In these verses Peter describes how the Christian should live according to God's great and precious promises and avoid the corruption of the world. He does so by mentioning the various virtues that characterize the lives of God's people.

The King James begins these verses with the words "And beside this, giving all diligence, add to…" The translation is inaccurate. It leaves the impression that the virtues that follow are unrelated to the foregoing. The idea is then that these virtues are merely in addition to and independent from the preceding context. This is not Peter's meaning.

In addition, the King James renders these verses as if the virtues themselves are unrelated one to the other. They are merely added to one another, piled, as it were, on top of each other but without connection. This is indicated by the word "add," which is stated in verse 5 and implied in the following verses: add to your faith virtue; (add) to your virtue knowledge; (add) to knowledge temperance, and so on.

A more accurate translation will make the meaning clear. It is preferable to render the first part of verse 5 as "For this very reason, make every effort to add to…" The question is, for what reason? The answer is found in verse 3: God has given us all things that pertain to life and godliness. The idea is that on the basis and for the reason that God has given us all things, we are to obey the admonitions that Peter spells out in the following verses.

Peter strengthens his reasoning by admonishing us to make every effort to add the virtues that characterize the Christian life. The words that he uses are interesting.

"All diligence" is "every effort." Peter places these words first in the sentence to give them emphasis; the words are intended to convey a sense of urgency and haste. We are not to spare any energy, but we must exert ourselves to the utmost to do what Peter enjoins. This idea is conveyed by "giving," which means that we are to be active in our salvation in the sense of Philippians 2:12–13: "Wherefore, my beloved, as ye have always obeyed, not as in my presence only, but now much more in my absence, work out your own salvation with fear and trembling. For it is God which worketh in you both to will and to do of his good pleasure."

The verb "add" comes from the ancient world of stage and drama, of which the Greeks were so fond. The government paid for part of the expenses of putting on a stage performance. The remainder of the cost was borne by the play's director, who therefore had a vested interest in the success of the performance. From a spiritual perspective, the meaning is that the believer is active in God's work of his salvation by living according to the virtues that Peter here enumerates. This obviously does not mean that living according to these virtues is a condition to salvation, as the Arminians teach, nor does it imply a form of works righteousness. Our living according to these virtues is in no way a matter of merit; salvation is only and always the work of God's grace through faith. But this does mean that God is pleased to make us active in our sanctification. We as Christians must and do participate in God's work of salvation within us. We have a vested interest in our salvation, as scripture everywhere teaches.

Peter next spells out the virtues that must characterize the Christian life. As noted previously, these virtues are not unrelated and unconnected; the links are not disparate. Rather, this list can be compared to a chain of eight links, beginning with faith and ending with love. To each of these links we must give attention.

The first and strongest link is "faith." Peter in verse 3 assumes the existence of faith. He starts with faith when he speaks of adding to faith virtue. Faith here is saving faith, the bond between us and Christ. It is the subjective connection by which we are united with Christ. It is the believer's trust in his Savior and therefore the basis of his spiritual life. It is the fundamental power and root without which all other virtues are impossible.

The second link is "virtue." Peter uses the same word he used in verse 3. It refers to God's essential goodness and holiness. As this is reflected in us, it is moral, ethical, spiritual goodness that manifests our faith by a godly life and walk. Our faith is not to be hidden under a bushel but must shine forth as the light of the world (Matt. 5:15–16).

The third link is "knowledge." The word means a precise and correct knowledge in an intellectual sense. This knowledge, therefore, is the apprehension of spiritual things in relation to our walk of virtue or goodness. Without the spiritual power of goodness or virtue, knowledge is impossible. It is possible to know and understand the truth intellectually without understanding it spiritually. It is only in the context of faith and goodness that true knowledge is possible. Knowledge in the correct, spiritual sense goes hand in hand with faith, so that faith is strengthened through knowledge, and knowledge is increased by faith. Knowledge in the context of faith is the weapon that opposes and defeats error and unbelief, fighting the battle of faith by the sword of the Spirit, which is the word of God (Eph. 6:17).

The fourth link is "temperance," better translated as self-control. In Peter's day the word was used in the context of sports, which were as popular or more popular (if that is possible) than they are today. The idea is that an athlete abstained from anything and everything that would compromise his ability to compete. The meaning is clear from the words of Paul in 1 Corinthians 9:25 (NIV): "Everyone who competes in the games goes into strict training." Peter, no doubt acquainted with Paul's writings, refers to the purpose of this strict training in the spiritual sense: "They do it to get a crown that will not last, but we do it to get a crown that will last forever."

Peter does not further define self-discipline but uses it in a general sense. This implies that we ought not fall into the trap of legalism, so that self-control consists of a series of do's and don'ts.

Rather, he and other apostles generally mention self-control as a spiritual virtue that believers must practice (Gal. 5:23; Titus 1:8).

The fifth link in the chain is "patience," better rendered as perseverance. The word means to remain under in the face of conflict and trouble, and thus to endure. It is the spiritual power by which we endure suffering for Christ's sake and are not deterred from our purpose to serve him despite the persecution to which we are subjected. Patience is linked with faith in the sense that with the other virtues, patience has its origin in faith. In addition, this patience is connected with self-control. It is only in the way of self-control that patience is possible.

The sixth link is "godliness." Godliness is the fear of God, not in the sense of being afraid of him, but in the sense of reverencing and respecting him and therefore being afraid to displease him by doing the evil that he forbids. Godliness is piety, not in a sickly, mystical way, but in the consciousness that we as mere creatures live in the presence of the sovereign God of heaven and earth. Godliness is connected with perseverance: only in the way of godliness is it possible to persevere and endure.

The seventh link is "brotherly kindness." Transliterated from the Greek, the word that Peter uses is *philadelphia*, which is literally "love of the brother." This word is restrictive. It refers only to brotherly affection among the saints, those who have like faith and who together live out of the principle of faith and who walk according to godliness. Between believers and unbelievers there is not and cannot be fraternal friendliness. Instead, there is antithesis between them. Positively, the godly must stick together as one family in close friendliness.

The eighth and final link is "charity," better translated as love. Peter uses the common and well-known word *agape*. Unlike the restrictive term "brotherly love," which is limited to believers and

to the church, *agape* is a broader concept. It is the love of knowledge and intelligence. In scripture the term is used often and in
many different ways, but here the apostle refers to the love of God
in our entire walk and life in the world. Everything we do must
be characterized by the love of God, whether it is toward God or
toward our fellow man. This love is the culmination of all the links
in Peter's chain and is the fruit of faith, the first link in the golden
chain of virtues.

Growth and Assurance
1:8–9

8. For if these things be in you, and abound, they make
   you that ye shall neither be barren nor unfruitful in the
   knowledge of our Lord Jesus Christ.
9. But he that lacketh these things is blind, and cannot see
   afar off, and hath forgotten that he was purged from his
   old sins.

In verses 8–11 Peter applies the chain of virtues so that we can
reap an abundant spiritual harvest in knowing Christ.

In verse 8 he begins by using "for," or because. Why must we as
Christians be characterized by the golden chain of virtues? Negatively, so that we are not unfruitful, and positively, so that we will
have an entrance into the kingdom of Christ.

Peter speaks of "these things," referring to the chain of virtues
he has just mentioned. If we possess these qualities, says the apostle, possessing them in superabundance, there will be a result. This
abundance will be that we will be neither barren nor unfruitful.
The words "barren" and "unfruitful" are synonymous in the King
James. "Barren" is better rendered as idle or inactive; the idea is that

one shuns labor that ought to be performed, and it has the connotation of being lazy. "Unfruitful" implies a plant or a tree that does not produce its expected fruit and is therefore useless.

Practicing the virtues Peter has mentioned has consequences. The result is that we are not idle or unfruitful in the knowledge of our Lord Jesus Christ. Peter states this truth somewhat negatively, but the implication is positive. The idea is that if we possess these virtues abundantly, they will prevent us from being spiritually ineffective and unproductive.

The apostle restates his point negatively in verse 9: he who lacks these things (the chain of virtues) is blind. Peter uses the figure of blindness. One who does not possess these things cannot see and understand spiritually. He cannot perceive the chain of virtues, much less live according to its elements.

Such a one cannot see afar off, says Peter. Literally, he is "myopic," that is, spiritually nearsighted. Just as one who has physical myopia cannot see well at a distance, so one who is affected with spiritual myopia cannot see the things of the future. He is spiritually so shortsighted that he cannot see past the end of his nose. He knows nothing of the chain of virtues. He can see only those things that are earthly and carnal, but not the things that are above. The result is that he lives a worldly life devoid of sanctification.

Peter goes on to say that he who is blind and myopic has forgotten that he has been purged from his old sins. The idea is that he has an attitude of forgetfulness that he has been cleansed from his past sins. He has spiritual amnesia regarding his sins and his sinful nature. Peter literally describes this as a "catharsis," a cleansing of the mind from the consciousness of sin, which is the missing of the mark of God's glory.

This cannot mean that once his sins were forgiven, but now they are not. God never retracts or cancels his forgiveness or his justification. Once forgiven is always forgiven, and once cleansed is always cleansed. There is never a falling away of the saints. Rather, the myopic amnesiac never was truly purged from his old sins. He professed to be cleansed; he claimed to have experienced forgiveness; he even appeared as if he was numbered with the forgiven. But he was not. He of whom Peter speaks forgets his forgiveness and ultimately manifests himself as an unbeliever. The result is that being blind and myopic, and forgetting that he was cleansed from sin, he still walks in a carnal and earthly sense.

Making Our Calling and Election Sure: 1:10–11

10. Wherefore the rather, brethren, give diligence to make your calling and election sure: for if ye do these things, ye shall never fall:
11. For so an entrance shall be ministered unto you abundantly into the everlasting kingdom of our Lord and Saviour Jesus Christ.

In the first part of verse 10 Peter draws a conclusion from what he has said in verse 9. "Wherefore" or therefore indicates a connective conclusion from the preceding. He adds the strong adversative conjunction "rather" in order to emphasize the difference between verses 9 and 10.

His admonition Peter directs toward his brethren, those who are related to him not by blood but by faith. To them he directs his admonition to make their calling and election sure. This must be a priority for God's people of all ages. When Peter speaks of giving diligence, he uses a word that means to exert oneself or to endeavor. We are to put forth every effort to make our calling and election sure, and we must hasten to do this.

Peter speaks of two elements of our salvation: calling and election.

God's calling is his sovereign work by which he addresses the sinner through the word of the gospel, calling him out of the darkness of sin and death into the light and life of his salvation in Christ. This calling is usually distinguished by Reformed theologians as an external and an internal calling. The external calling is the general or promiscuous proclamation of the gospel to all who hear it. The internal calling is the work of God's grace in the hearts of God's people through the Holy Spirit by which he applies the gospel to them, thus effectually calling them from darkness to light (2 Thess. 2:13–14): "But we are bound to give thanks alway to God for you, brethren beloved of the Lord, because God hath from the beginning chosen you to salvation through sanctification of the Spirit and belief of the truth: whereunto he called you by our gospel, to the obtaining of the glory of our Lord Jesus Christ." In 2 Peter 1:10 it is this internal calling that receives the emphasis.

This calling can be further distinguished. Negatively, it is a calling from or out of sin, guilt, and death, as Peter writes in 1 Peter 2:9: "But ye are a chosen generation, a royal priesthood, an holy nation, a peculiar people; that ye should shew forth the praises of him who hath called you out of darkness into his marvellous light." Positively, it is a calling to salvation and its many facets: holiness (1 Thess. 4:7); peace (1 Cor. 7:15); and the blessedness of the Lamb's marriage supper (Rev. 19:9). This positive aspect is emphasized here: we are to make our calling sure—not only our calling through the message of the gospel, but also our internal calling whereby the Holy Spirit applies to our hearts and lives the word of the gospel.

In harmony with the truth of the calling, Peter also speaks of our election. The word most commonly used in scripture for election means to pick out or to choose. Based on this meaning, election is the act of God's free will whereby from eternity he decreed his salvation to certain persons (but not to others) through Christ by grace alone. Stated similarly, election is God's eternal and sovereign decree to lead the church to eternal salvation and glory.

Peter teaches the truth of sovereign, double predestination, one of the salient truths of the Reformed faith. While he does not specifically mention reprobation but only election, reprobation (a truth almost universally denied and hated) is necessarily implied in election. If only some are chosen and elected, others are not and are rejected.

A word must be said concerning the order in which Peter mentions election and calling. In Romans 8:29–30, often considered to be the definitive order of salvation, the order of the calling and election is reversed: first is foreknowledge and predestination; second is the calling. How is this apparent contradiction of order to be explained? Is not election followed by the calling through the word of the gospel applied internally in our hearts by the word of the Holy Spirit? Is not the decree of election first, followed by the decree of the calling?

From the viewpoint of the logical order of God's decrees, election precedes the calling. God first elects his people in Christ from eternity, and those whom he predestinates he also calls. However, in the text Peter views calling and election not from the standpoint of God's decrees, but from man's perspective. Peter emphasizes the calling by placing it first. The idea is that by experiencing his calling, the believer is assured of his election.

Peter admonishes us to make our calling and election sure, that is, to make it stable and firm, without contradiction or weakness. How do we do this? By doing "these things," that is, the virtues that make up the chain of salvation he has already described. When these characterize believers and when we practice them, they are so many proofs of our calling and election.

In so doing we will never stumble or fall. Never will we doubt our calling and election. The believer is firmly established and is absolutely sure of his salvation. Never can he lose it.

In verse 11 the apostle says, "For so," that is, in the way of making our calling and election sure, we will receive a rich welcome into the eternal kingdom of our Lord and Savior Jesus Christ. What a wonderful promise! Peter uses the complete description of God's Son. He is Jesus, salvation; he is Christ, the Messiah; he is the savior, the one who redeems us; and he is the lord, the ruler of his people by grace both in time and in eternity.

Besides, Peter uses the singular "you" to express that our possession of Christ's kingdom is not an abstract concept, but it is personally ours.

The everlasting kingdom of which Peter speaks is the kingdom of our Lord and Savior. It is the everlasting kingdom because it is God's kingdom, for God is the sovereign and absolute ruler over all things—over all creation, over the wicked, and over the righteous. The emphasis falls not on God's kingdom of power (which it is), but on the heavenly kingdom of grace through Christ, which is why Peter uses the full and descriptive name of his Son to indicate God's full salvation of his elect people. He is the one who is our savior, the one who redeems his people from the death grip of sin, for he is Jesus, Jehovah salvation, and Christ, the anointed Messiah sent by the Father to redeem his people. Because he is the savior, Jesus Christ, he is also lord of his people, their sovereign who rules by grace over them eternally.

Peter's Concern for the Church: 1:12–15

12. Wherefore I will not be negligent to put you always in remembrance of these things, though ye know them, and be established in the present truth.
13. Yea, I think it meet, as long as I am in this tabernacle, to stir you up by putting you in remembrance;
14. Knowing that shortly I must put off this my tabernacle, even as our Lord Jesus Christ hath shewed me.
15. Moreover I will endeavour that ye may be able after my decease to have these things always in remembrance.

In these verses Peter changes from his doctrinal admonitions to a personal concern for the church to whom he writes. He introduces his comments by "wherefore," by which he draws a conclusion from what he has already written.

He begins in verse 12 by saying that he will not be negligent or careless to remind his readers or to put them in remembrance of "these things." Once again Peter refers to the virtues that comprise the chain of salvation (vv. 5–7). His phraseology is negative: he will not be negligent to remind God's people of these things. The reason is that we are often so caught up in our busy lives that we forget to be mindful of these things. Besides, we fail to remember these things because of the power of sin in our lives that leads us to forget them.

Peter's positive implication is that he does put the saints in remembrance of these things. He does so although his readers already know these truths. They are established or stable in the present truth of the gospel. There is no doubt that they are confirmed in it. They know not an obsolete or outdated truth, much less a false gospel, but the truth being presently taught by Peter and the other apostles. The content of Peter's letter is then a reminder of the truth of God's revelation from Peter's personal ("I") viewpoint, which indicates his love for the church.

Peter continues in verse 13 by telling the church that he thinks it is right or appropriate for him to stir them up or to wake them up by giving them this reminder. A reminder of what? A reminder of everything that Peter has taught in the preceding verses, specifically the chain of salvation described in 1:5–7. Never should they forget what they have learned. Why does Peter think it necessary to issue this reminder?

The first reason is that we are prone to spiritual forgetfulness. It is so easy to fall asleep and fail to be alert in the battle of faith that constantly rages around us. If we are spiritually drowsy, we cannot participate in the war.

The second reason is that Peter knows that his death is imminent. In verse 13 he expresses this by saying "as long as I am in this tabernacle." In verse 14 he says, "Knowing that shortly I must put off this my tabernacle." When speaking in these verses of his tabernacle, Peter uses a word that means tent. By this metaphor he refers to his earthly existence. He speaks of himself in terms of a tabernacle, an obvious reference to the Old Testament tabernacle, which was a tent, a fact with which his readers surely were familiar. The figure is instructive. A tent is a temporary dwelling in contrast with the permanence of a house.

Peter uses poetic language to emphasize that he soon will die. He conveys a sense of urgency by saying that his death will occur shortly. Lest his readers should conclude that he simply has a morbid preoccupation with his death or is merely expressing an unfounded opinion, he informs them that the Lord Jesus Christ has showed him that his life is nearly over.

It cannot be ascertained how the Lord showed that to Peter, and he does not tell us. However, because the canon of scripture was not yet closed at that time, leaving the door open to direct revelation, it seems likely that God spoke through the Holy Spirit personally to Peter.

More important is Peter's assertion in verse 15 that he will endeavor so that after his death God's people would be able to have these things—what he has taught them, specifically the chain of salvation—in remembrance. He uses the same word as in verse 10: I will exert myself and make every effort to make sure that this happens. He will do this in light of his decease, literally his "exodus," which implies the close of his apostolic career and his departure from this life.

What is Peter's reason for stressing his imminent death? His urgency is that he will no longer be present to teach the church, but God's people must after his demise remember the authority and importance of his teaching. This sense of urgency drives the apostle to put his teaching in written form in his epistles, specifically the present letter.

The Authority and Truthfulness of Peter's Teaching: 1:16–18

16. For we have not followed cunningly devised fables, when we made known unto you the power and coming of our Lord Jesus Christ, but were eyewitnesses of his majesty.
17. For he received from God the Father honour and glory, when there came such a voice to him from the excellent glory, This is my beloved Son, in whom I am well pleased.
18. And this voice which came from heaven we heard, when we were with him in the holy mount.

In these verses Peter defends what he has been teaching the church. He does this (v. 16) "for," or because, he wants God's people to understand that they must believe what he has reminded them. In so doing, he switches from the personal singular pronoun "I" to the personal plural "we." By the plural pronoun Peter includes himself with the other apostles.

Peter asserts that he and his fellow apostles did not follow cunningly devised fables when they made known the power and coming of the Lord Jesus Christ. Fables are myths. A myth is a fictional story, a tale that has little or no basis in reality. It is therefore a falsehood. The apostle further describes these fables as cunningly devised or cleverly invented. In his day especially the Greeks were experts at devising and producing elaborate myths, particularly concerning their pantheon of gods. The Greeks were so clever that they made their fables appear to be the truth.

Such myths, Peter says, he and the other apostles have not believed or followed when they made known to the church the power and coming of Christ. In no way is the teaching of the gospel to be put into the same category as the heathen myths. Here the coming of Christ means his *parousia*, the term universally used in the New Testament to refer not to his first advent, but to his second and final coming as it is described primarily in the book of Revelation. This coming will be powerful (the same word used in verse 3), which means that it will accomplish what God intends—the salvation of his people, the destruction of the wicked, and the renewal of all things (Matt. 24:30; Mark 9:1).

Peter speaks of the final revelation of Christ's power and coming. But in the last part of verse 16, when he asserts that the apostles were eyewitnesses of Christ's majesty, he refers to the prefiguration of the final coming in Jesus' transfiguration during his earthly ministry (Matt. 17:1–8). In a general sense all twelve of the disciples, later the apostles, were eyewitnesses of Jesus during the time they followed him, heard his teaching, and witnessed his miracles, in which his divine power flashed through the darkness of the sin-cursed world; they were also witnesses of his post-resurrection appearances, in which his divine glory was clearly evident. But neither of those is the meaning of this verse. Rather, the reference is to the transfiguration.

In a unique way Peter, James, and John were the only disciples who were eyewitnesses of the transfiguration. By the time this epistle was written James was dead, but Peter and John were not, and therefore Peter could speak authoritatively as to what he saw. Peter identifies Christ's transfiguration as his majesty (v. 16). Majesty is magnificence or splendor, which fits well with Matthew's description that "his face did shine as the sun, and his raiment was white as the light" (Matt. 17:2). "Honor" has the connotation of reverence, and "glory" refers to the manifestation of the splendor and brightness of God's perfections (2 Pet. 1:17). This honor and glory were given by the Father, so that on the mount Christ, according to his human nature, was partaker of the glory of the triune God. Such is Peter's characterization of the visual aspect of the transfiguration.

This visual transformation was confirmed by God's verbal approval of his Son: "This is my beloved Son, in whom I am well pleased" (v. 17). It is noteworthy that the word Peter uses for "beloved" has as its root the well-known word used in the New Testament for love—*agape*. The word indicates a deep and abiding love like the love between husband and wife. The object of this love is esteemed above all else, so that the text can be rendered, "This is my dearly loved Son."

The question arises, why does Peter bring up and emphasize Christ's transfiguration? The answer is twofold.

The first reason lies in the idea of "eyewitnesses" in verse 16.

In order for the disciples to write their gospel narratives and the various epistles as apostles after Christ's ascension, they had to be firsthand witnesses of the teachings and miracles of Jesus and of all aspects of his life and work. The disciples/apostles were eyewitnesses of Christ in his state of humiliation—his lowly birth, his suffering, his death, his descent into hell, and his burial. They were also witnesses of his resurrection and ascension. But never—except for the transfiguration—were they witnesses of Christ's future power and glory in his second coming. Thus we see the necessity of the glimpse Jesus gave to his disciples of his future glory in the new creation, and thus Peter emphasizes the transfiguration. They had to be witnesses of the complete work of the Savior.

The second reason must be found in the juxtaposition of "we… were eyewitnesses" (v. 16b) and "this voice which came from heaven we heard" (v. 18) with "we have not followed cunningly devised fables" (v. 16a). Peter anticipates the accusation of the wicked reprobate that the gospel he preaches and writes is nothing more than another cleverly invented myth. In contrast, Peter asserts antithetically that he and the other apostles have seen Christ's future glory and have heard God's approval of his Son. His assertion is that his gospel is completely credible.

A More Sure Word of Prophecy: 1:19–21

19. We have also a more sure word of prophecy; whereunto ye do well that ye take heed, as unto a light that shineth in a dark place, until the day dawn, and the day star arise in your hearts:
20. Knowing this first, that no prophecy of the scripture is of any private interpretation.

21. For the prophecy came not in old time by the will of man: but holy men of God spake as they were moved by the Holy Ghost.

Peter continues by stating that the church to which he writes has "a more sure word of prophecy." Prophecy refers not first and primarily to the predicting of the future, but to the word of God as spoken and written by Peter and the other apostles concerning the coming of the Lord. This prophecy is "sure," that is, it is firm and trustworthy. It is "more" sure because it is the prophecy concerning the power and coming of the Lord as it is prefigured in the transfiguration, as witnessed by Peter, James, and John ("we"), and as rejected by cunningly devised myths. The word of prophecy is therefore the corroboration of the parousia by the transfiguration.

Peter goes on to advise the church to take heed or to pay attention to the sure word of prophecy because it is to their benefit to do so. The apostle then resorts to figurative language to make his point.

First, he compares the sure word of prophecy to a light, a lamp or a candle, that shines in a dark place. The word that he uses does not mean the blackness of the night but refers to a dim and dingy place. This squalid place is the world as it is under the dominion of sin and the curse, as it is dismally hopeless and destitute of brightness. In this world the light of the word of prophecy, the brightness of prophecy, shines like a beacon light, proclaiming the future glory and light of the church's final glory through the return of Christ, the destruction of the dark place, and the establishment of the new creation.

Second, Peter instructs the church to believe the sure word of prophecy "until the day dawn[s]." Peter speaks not of the fullness of the day, not of the complete redemption of all things in the glory of the new and eternal creation, but of the dawning of the day. Of this Christ's transfiguration, as confirmation of his future glorification, and the sure word of prophecy are figures. The day is not yet. But as the dawn breaks across the dark skies of sin, the curse, and death, the promise of full redemption is near. Even now the light of final salvation glimmers through the night in anticipation of the full glory of the day.

Third, Peter compares the word of prophecy to the rising of the day star in the hearts of God's elect people. This is a wonderfully descriptive figure. The day star, also called the bright and morning star in Revelation 22:16 with reference to Christ, is Venus, the planet that just before dawn appears in the eastern sky as the harbinger of the rising of the sun. When the morning star shines in the east, the full glory of the sun soon follows. The exact reference of this figure is difficult to determine, but it seems that the coming of the sign of the Son of man (Matt. 24:30) is the meaning here. This rising of the day star takes place also in the hearts of God's people. Because they believe the word of prophecy, they recognize the rising of the dawn as the beginning of their final glorification by God through Christ.

Peter defines in verse 20 what prophecy is *not*. The prophecy of scripture, regardless of what prophecy, is never of anyone's private interpretation or analysis. When prophecy has been given and spoken, it is impossible for the prophet who spoke it to give a detailed interpretation or a clear fulfillment of the words he has spoken. One of the aspects of prophecy is the prediction of future events. But the prophets themselves could not interpret their own words except as they were given the understanding of them by the Holy Spirit.

Peter further explains his point in verse 21 by asserting negatively that the prophecy of scripture did not come "in old time by the will of man," and positively that "holy men of God spake as they were moved by the Holy Ghost." The prophecy of old time is the Old Testament scripture, although the principle stated in this verse applies also to prophecy in the New Testament, which was at that time still in the process of being written. This prophecy did not come or was not conveyed by the will of man. Peter's actual statement is that prophecy *never* originates from the will of man. This is an absolute impossibility. It is also the reason for what is said in verse 20, "that no prophecy...is of any private interpretation." For that reason it was not given by the will of man.

By way of a positive contrast, Peter teaches that holy men of God spoke as they were moved by the Holy Spirit. This is one of the clearest proofs that can be found for the inspiration of scripture. It is also the death of all compromise of this doctrine. Contrary to the teaching of many, including some purportedly Reformed theologians, there is not a primary author (God) of scripture and a secondary author (man). Nor is there a divine and a human factor in the speaking and writing of prophecy. Rather, the Holy Spirit is the one and only author of all scripture, while men are the writers, the instruments whom God is pleased to use to produce his word (Belgic Confession 3). These men are called holy not because they are personally perfect, but because God has sanctified and prepared them to write the scriptures. Thus they are men *from* God, that is, they were men sent from God, and they spoke and wrote from God. It is the Holy Spirit who moved those men as the wind carries a ship along, a descriptive figure that explains inspiration.

With this doctrine the first chapter of 2 Peter ends.

CHAPTER **TWO**

False Teachers:
Their Heresies: 2:1

1. But there were false prophets also among the people, even as there shall be false teachers among you, who privily shall bring in damnable heresies, even denying the Lord that bought them, and bring upon themselves swift destruction.

In chapter 1, Peter's message to the church was overwhelmingly positive. The only significant exception was his mention of cunningly devised fables. However, in chapter 2 his message is universally negative as he describes the false prophets and false teachers who have plagued and still do plague the church. His description of these false teachers—ministers and other influential members—must be understood on two levels.

First, these teachers are already present in the early New Testament church to which Peter writes. They are therefore a present danger of which the church must beware.

Second, the apostle also writes of a future aspect. In several instances he uses the future tense in describing false teachers. This implies that the problem of false teachers not only existed in Peter's day, but will also continue throughout the New Testament and will even increase and worsen as the end of time approaches. By implication he warns the church against these heretics, present both in his time and in his perspective of the future.

It should not be overlooked that the apostle speaks of both pseudo-prophets and pseudo-teachers. The difference is not one of essence but of equivalence and emphasis. In that both prophets and teachers are those who reveal the word of God to his people, there is no essential difference between them. But in that prophets in the Old Testament were to a lesser or a greater extent concerned with and prophesied concerning the future, while teachers in the New Testament are concerned with instructing the church in the word already revealed, there is indeed a difference of emphasis. Prophets belong to the Old Testament, teachers to the New. Thus Peter uses the past tense in mentioning false prophets and the present or future tense when speaking of false teachers.

In verse 1 Peter introduces the subject of false teachers in the church. He calls them pseudo-teachers, that is, those who are fakes, those who pretend to speak the word of God but in reality do not.

False prophets existed often in the history of Israel (think of the numerous prophets of Baal at the time of Elijah). Peter's focus, however, is not primarily on the past, but on the teachers of the present and of the future. He uses examples from the past, as we will see, but he does so only to prove his point regarding the church of his day.

Peter says that the false teachers will privily bring in damnable heresies. By his use of the future tense he warns the church of what will soon happen. These teachers will not be clear and forthright in their teachings but will secretly sneak them into the church. "Damnable" in our usage means worthy of condemnation, and this is basically correct. The word means destruction and refers to perdition, a loss of eternal life, and eternal misery.

Such heresies are worthy of eternal damnation. Why does Peter use such blunt language? Because he is Peter, blunt of character and speech, but essentially because he recognizes the terribly destructive character of the heresies introduced into the church by the false teachers.

Their heresy brings on them swift destruction. In speaking of destruction, Peter uses the word translated as "damnable" earlier in the verse. This destruction is swift and unexpected. Just when the false teachers think they are getting away with promulgating their heresies unopposed, sudden destruction from God comes upon them. The examples of Noah and of Sodom and Gomorrah later in the chapter are evidence of Peter's point.

False Teachers:
Their Pernicious Ways: 2:2–3

2. And many shall follow their pernicious ways; by reason of whom the way of truth shall be evil spoken of.
3. And through covetousness shall they with feigned words make merchandise of you: whose judgment now of a long time lingereth not, and their damnation slumbereth not.

The result of the activity of the false teachers is twofold: many will follow their pernicious ways, and the way of truth will be blasphemed. The "many" are the members of the church who are deceived by the false teachers. Not all follow them, but significantly, many, often a majority, do; the history of the church from earliest times bears witness to this fact.

The ways of false teachers are "pernicious," that is, shameful, characterized by unbridled lust, wantonness, and carnality. Peter is not specific as to the exact nature of what constitutes their ways, but it seems reasonable from the meaning of this word that their teaching is man centered rather than God centered. This is evident from the entire history of the church. The issue is always this: is salvation the work of God or the work of man? The false teachers give the wrong answer in order to enhance their own carnal interests, perhaps by promoting themselves, as does the Roman Catholic hierarchy.

The result is that because of them the way of truth is evil spoken of, literally "blasphemed" or causing disrepute to the church. A "way" in scripture, sometimes called conversation, is the path along which the church travels in relationship to the wicked world. The world always watches the church to see if its external walk is consistent with its doctrine or teaching. When the church's manifestation and conduct are inconsistent with its teachings, the world has occasion to blaspheme and reject the way of truth in which the church should walk but does not. Only when the church walks in the way of truth (Ps. 119:30) are the mouths of the world stopped.

What is the motive of false teachers? Peter says that it is "covetousness" or greed and desire for gain. They want to be popular, which often translates into greed and the desire to accumulate riches through their supposed teaching of the gospel. The televangelists who in our day promote a health and wealth gospel are clear examples of this, especially when their avarice is exposed.

These teachers use "feigned words" to accomplish their greedy goals. This is what Peter means when he writes that they make merchandise of the believers. Making merchandise means to use someone or something for gain, to exploit someone, which is exactly what the false teachers do. They do this by using feigned words.

"Feigned" means molded and is the term from which we derive our word *plastic*. Plastic is flexible and easily molded according to the desire of its maker or user. The false teachers use plastic words. They mold their teachings to fit the situation, telling their hearers what they want to hear instead of uncompromisingly teaching the gospel of the scriptures.

The false teachers, however, will not go unpunished. Peter describes this in two clauses reminiscent of Hebrew parallelism. Parallelism is a literary device in which the same idea is expressed in two similar ways, with the second clause explaining the first. Literally he writes in verse 3, "Whose judgment of old is not lingering, and whose destruction is not sleeping."

The judgment of the first clause is judgment in the negative sense of condemnation, since it is parallel with the destruction (damnation) of the second clause. This judgment is from of old; it has been impending for a long time. It has been hanging over their heads, although they have not seen it coming. The parallel idea in the second clause is that their destruction (the same word used twice in verse 1) has not been nodding off to sleep.

Judgment has various shades of meaning, as it does here. There is judgment in God's counsel, the working out of his eternal and sovereign decree of reprobation. There is also the sudden and final judgment at the end of time. There is also a judgment in time, and this is the emphasis here. Judgment does not occur instantaneously but is executed by God in the way of sin. As Romans 1 teaches, sin breeds sin and is its own judgment. In this way the false teachers and those who follow them become prepared for their final judgment. Their judgment does not tarry, and their destruction does not slumber but is wide awake, so that they are rushing to their ultimate catastrophe from which they cannot escape.

False Teachers: Three Examples of Their Certain Destruction: 2:4–8

4. For if God spared not the angels that sinned, but cast them down to hell, and delivered them into chains of darkness, to be reserved unto judgment;

5. And spared not the old world, but saved Noah the eighth person, a preacher of righteousness, bringing in the flood upon the world of the ungodly;

6. And turning the cities of Sodom and Gomorrha into ashes condemned them with an overthrow, making them an ensample unto those that after should live ungodly;

7. And delivered just Lot, vexed with the filthy conversation of the wicked:

8. (For that righteous man dwelling among them, in seeing and hearing, vexed his righteous soul from day to day with their unlawful deeds;)

Peter gives three examples from the Old Testament to demonstrate that God judges those who oppose him, while protecting and preserving his church from false teachers. In so doing, his intent is to assure the church that God's judgment on false teachers is swift and sure, while he saves his elect people. False teachers may attempt to deceive the church; they may make merchandise of God's people; they may blaspheme the church. Yet God always saves the righteous and destroys the wicked.

His first example is that of the wicked angels. The world of angels and their fall is a subject about which we do not know very much because angels belong to the spirit world, while scripture is concerned primarily with events in our world, particularly creation, the fall, and the redemption of man. God created the angels as perfect, spiritual beings to praise him and to do his will (for instance, Gabriel, his announcing angel, and Michael the arch-angel, leader of the righteous angels against Satan). But some of the angels sinned and fell prior to Adam's fall and just as Adam became wicked servants of Satan, the ultimate evil being opposed to God and his cause. Peter does not tell us the nature of the angels' sin because this is not his point, but it seems likely that they rebelled against God because in pride they wanted to be like him, knowing good and evil (Gen. 3:5).

Because the angels sinned, God did not spare them but sent them down to hell. Peter uses the word *Tartarus*, a mythical Greek god and a part of hell where most of the wicked are kept to receive divine judgment. The use of this term does not mean that Peter endorsed pagan mythology. Rather, he uses this descriptive term because it was familiar to his readers, who surely were acquainted with the Greek idolatry of that day. Hell is a dark and doleful place, a place of suffering and punishment. There God sent the disobedi-ent angels to await their final judgment in the day of the Lord.

In addition, God delivered the fallen angels into "chains of darkness, to be reserved unto judgment." The figurative expression "chains of darkness" means that those angels are forever kept in the gloom of hell. They are bound by their sin, and for them there is no hope of escape from their bondage of sin. They will be tor-mented forever and ever (Rev. 20:10). During the history of time, they will be guarded so that they are unable to slip their chains and wreak havoc on the church. At the end of time, some angels will be allowed temporarily to roam the earth and to seek the destruction of the church, but this is not Peter's focus. He is concerned only with the judgment and condemnation of those wicked creatures.

The second example of the judgment of the false teachers is

that of Noah and the flood. The first example of the angels was only the revelation of God's judgment; this second example shows both God's wrath against the wicked and his salvation of his people. The contrast serves to emphasize his point.

Peter says in verse 5 that God "spared not the old world" when he brought the flood upon the world of the ungodly. His reference is obviously to the ancient world that existed from creation to the flood, which world was very different from our world. That world was overwhelmingly inhabited by the ungodly, the impious who had no reverential awe toward God but persisted and developed in their godless ways. Genesis describes the situation unequivocally:

5. And God saw that the wickedness of man was great in the earth, and that every imagination of the thoughts of his heart was only evil continually…

11. The earth also was corrupt before God, and the earth was filled with violence.

12. And God looked upon the earth, and, behold, it was corrupt; for all flesh had corrupted his way upon the earth (6:5, 11–12).

The wicked world was ripe for destruction; man's total depravity had manifested itself in the development of sin and the filling of the cup of iniquity.

That world God did not spare. Perhaps we could think that God would preserve it for the sake of his church, represented by Noah and his family, but that was not so. The negative expression that he spared not the old world serves to emphasize that he destroyed it completely.

Peter calls the flood a cataclysm. A cataclysm is a total and unmitigated disaster. Such was the flood. It was not merely a lengthy and heavy rainstorm, but the heavens were opened, the fountains of the great deep were broken up, all men and all living creatures were destroyed, and the nature of the entire earthly creation was altered. All of the details are not pertinent here. Peter's point is that the judgment of God on the wicked world was universal and cataclysmic.

In the midst of that total disaster, only Noah and his family were saved. He is called "the eighth person," a reference to the other seven members of his family: his wife, his three sons, and their wives. These eight constituted all that remained of the church immediately before the flood.

In the midst of this environment, Noah was a preacher of righteousness. "Preacher" means a herald or messenger, one who speaks on behalf of another. This accurately describes Noah's function. He was the representative of God in the wicked world, the one who spoke the word that he had been given to proclaim. The content of his preaching was righteousness. Even more, he was one of the few righteous remaining in the universally wicked world of his day. That Noah was a preacher of righteousness means that he testified concerning God's righteousness and man's obligation to be righteous as God is righteous and therefore to serve him. The negative implication is that Noah in his preaching condemned the wickedness of the world, warning the unbelievers of the coming cataclysm and commanding them to repent and believe. As we know from the history, the world refused to believe and instead mocked Noah for building a floating zoo on dry land, thus incurring the wrath of God, while Noah and his seven were saved by the waters of the flood.

If God did not spare the old world, how will he spare the false teachers, who as the wicked of old oppose the church and seek to lead it away from the truth? Such is Peter's point in the example of the flood. Yet God will preserve believers, just as he protected Noah from the most tremendous catastrophe in the history of the world. Peter's intention therefore is to encourage the church to which he writes.

The third example of the judgment of false teachers is that of Sodom and Gomorrah. These cities are examples of the ultimate manifestation of wickedness, according to Romans 1. Those cities were not just sinful in general, but their inhabitants were noteworthy for their sin of homosexuality, which even today is proverbial. All of the historical details of those cities are not Peter's point here. Rather, he emphasizes that Sodom and Gomorrah were so full of iniquity that they were ripe for judgment. In this they are typical of the final judgment; sin must develop organically until it bears its full fruit and is then ready for judgment.

Therefore, God burned the cities to ashes. He condemned them by overthrowing and destroying them, raining fire and sulfur upon them. This is Peter's point: he compares the condemnation of the false teachers to the utter destruction of Sodom and Gomorrah. This ought to be a warning to all false teachers.

Lot was the exception to this destruction. Again, all of the details are not the main idea. Nevertheless, Lot is pictured as the exception to the destruction of those cities. Twice he is described as a righteous man (2:8). However, he was morally and spiritually weak. He separated from Abraham and from the covenant, and he chose for carnal reasons to dwell in Sodom. Yet Peter does not dwell on Lot's weaknesses but instead mentions that in observing the wickedness around him, Lot continually vexed his righteous soul. He tormented or tortured himself, undoubtedly because of the foolish choice he had made in living in Sodom and being forced to watch the sins committed by its wicked inhabitants. He was distressed by the lascivious conduct of those among whom he lived and undoubtedly condemned their filthy conversation, that is, their walk and lifestyle of depravity.

God saved Lot. He had to send angels to accomplish this, and in the process Lot lost most of his family. But when destruction came upon Sodom and Gomorrah, the ultimate result was Lot's salvation. Peter's point is that while God visits utter destruction on the wicked, as he will do to the false teachers, he always saves his people, also from false teachers.

False Teachers: Assurance against Them: 2:9–10a

9. The Lord knoweth how to deliver the godly out of temptations, and to reserve the unjust unto the day of judgment to be punished:

10a. But chiefly them that walk after the flesh in the lust of uncleanness, and despise government.

From the three examples of the angels, Noah, and Lot, Peter in these verses draws a conclusion. Based on his examples, he teaches that the Lord knows how to deliver the godly while punishing the wicked. This may not always seem to be true. It may appear as if the wicked sin with impunity, that the situation of the righteous is hopeless, and that the cause of the church is doomed to failure. Nevertheless, Peter in these verses contradicts this thinking and instead sets forth a general truth.

This principle is that the Lord knows how to deliver the godly out of temptation and to punish the wicked in the day of judgment. The principle has two aspects.

Positively, in the face of the likely despondence of God's people because their cause is apparently doomed, Peter assures them that God knows how to deliver them. He speaks of the godly, that is, of the righteous, those who serve God, those who do not follow false teachers. They are tempted, however, by the false teachings of the unrighteous, and this constitutes for them a trial of their faith. But the Lord knows how to sustain them in this trial and gives them the ability to resist this temptation. Peter's point is not just that the Lord knows how to rescue them but does nothing. His meaning is that because God knows how to deliver, he actually does so. This is evident from the fact that Peter calls God "the Lord," emphasizing that God is the sovereign ruler over all things.

Negatively, God knows how to reserve the unjust unto the day of judgment to be punished. The unjust are the unrighteous, those whose teaching and walk of life are contrary to the scriptures, whom Peter has already begun to describe. God reserves them, that is, continually guards and controls them until the final judgment at the end of time. He as it were holds their eternal judgment over their heads, and in the final judgment the weight of their ultimate condemnation will fall upon them in the everlasting destruction of hell. Meanwhile he punishes them. The word that Peter uses is literally "to trim" or "to prune" and thus means that the unjust are cut off from the truth and from the church, pending their final destruction.

This principle that Peter sets forth is based on his three previous antithetical examples. Many angels fell because of their rebellion, but some did not. The entire world was destroyed in the flood, but Noah and his seven were saved. Sodom and Gomorrah were destroyed, but Lot was preserved.

The apostle's point, although not directly stated, is the assurance of God's people that their salvation is sure despite all the efforts of the wicked to destroy the church. The implication is the comfort and assurance of God's people.

Peter singles out ("chiefly") those who "walk after the flesh in the lust of uncleanness, and despise government." The term *flesh* in scripture can refer to man's physical existence in the sense that he is flesh and blood, but this is not the primary meaning here. Rather, flesh has an ethical meaning: flesh in contrast to and opposed to spirit. Flesh is the whole nature of man from the viewpoint of his existence apart from God. It is man's sinful, totally depraved nature, his proneness to sin, and his rejection of and rebellion against God. According to the flesh is how these wicked live and make their way during their earthly sojourns.

In walking after the flesh, the false teachers also walk "in the lust of uncleanness." Lust is a strong desire, usually used in scripture in a negative sense of a craving for that which is forbidden. Usually when lust is mentioned, the first thing that comes to mind is lust in an illicit sexual sense. While there may be some justification for this, the meaning is more general, including any desire for what is proscribed. Here, however, the emphasis seems to fall on sexual sins, since the false teachers were apparently using their positions as leaders to take sexual advantage of their followers.

This interpretation is reinforced by the meaning of "uncleanness." From this term we derive the English word *miasma*, a haze of defilement or a fog of pollution, which graphically describes the influence of false teachers.

They also despise government. The term does not refer first to secular government, although this is certainly included, because God rules over such governments. Instead, it refers to the dominion of divine authority. God is undeniably sovereign, but they deny his lordship, substituting their own authority for his.

False Teachers: Their Sins: 2:10b–16

10b. Presumptuous are they, self-willed, they are not afraid to speak evil of dignities.

11. Whereas angels, which are greater in power and might, bring not railing accusation against them before the Lord.

12. But these, as natural brute beasts, made to be taken and destroyed, speak evil of the things that they understand not; and shall utterly perish in their own corruption;

13. And shall receive the reward of unrighteousness, as they that count it pleasure to riot in the day time. Spots they are and blemishes, sporting themselves with their own deceivings while they feast with you;

14. Having eyes full of adultery, and that cannot cease from sin; beguiling unstable souls: an heart they have exercised with covetous practices; cursed children:

15. Which have forsaken the right way, and are gone astray, following the way of Balaam the son of Bosor, who loved the wages of unrighteousness;

16. But was rebuked for his iniquity: the dumb ass speaking with man's voice forbad the madness of the prophet.

At this point Peter launches into a lengthy description of false teachers in terms of their sins. Their first sin is blasphemy. Peter says that they are "presumptuous," that is, daring. They do not hesitate to contradict the word of God. They are also "self-willed," arrogantly pleasing themselves. Their concern is not for the church, but for their own benefit and advancement.

They are so cocky and self-confident that they are not even afraid "to speak evil of dignitaries" (v. 10). The correct translation is that they "are not afraid to blaspheme glories."

Peter's teaching is that heretics are so bold and arrogant that they are unafraid of slandering dignities, literally glories. Peter does not define in detail the identity of dignities, but the reference is doubtless to all those who are in positions of power and authority, esteem and reputation, and who are therefore worthy of respect, obedience, and praise. These glories would then include the apostles, together with others in positions of leadership and authority in the church (see 1 Cor. 12:28; 2 Cor. 8:23). Surely the righteous angels, glorious as they are, fit this description. The term even extends to those in authority in the earthly and civil realm, what scripture calls the magistrates.

Regarding these glories the heretics do not hesitate to speak evil. They take to themselves a judgment that belongs only to God and show no respect toward the dignities. They hurl insults (blasphemous judgments) against them. They speak slanderous and abusive words against the glories. The problem is that they do not know what they are talking about (2 Pet. 2:12), and that their speech is driven by their wicked hearts and minds.

Their speaking about things "that they understand not" (v. 12), literally "without the word," that is, without the truth of the word of God, proves that they are false teachers. In speaking of what they know nothing about, they are literally "agnostic"—those who are without knowledge, those who know nothing about God. They are not different from natural brute beasts, creatures governed not by reason but by instinct. Their existence is only physical, in the here and now, and in no way spiritual. What a scathing comparison! False teachers are compared with brute beasts!

Peter goes on to write that they are made to be taken and destroyed, that is, God's purpose is that they are captured like an animal in a trap, so that they will be destroyed (v. 12) and so that he may show his power and glory in them. Their end is that they utterly perish in their own corruption. Peter writes literally, "In their destroying they are also destroyed." The false teachers themselves are destroyed while they destroy the church, corrupt the truth, and blaspheme things concerning which they have no knowledge.

The false teachers will "receive the reward of unrighteousness" (v. 13). Peter uses a play on words and says that they will suffer wrong as the wages of doing wrong. The idea is that of divine recompense; they will receive the wages they have earned by their iniquity. Their punishment will be eternal suffering in hell.

In the remainder of verse 13 Peter continues his unflattering description of false teachers and their evil conduct. They count it a pleasure to riot in the day time. "Riot" can be better translated as living softly or luxuriously, and thus to carouse. Drunkenness is certainly implied, perhaps accompanied by gluttony and sexual immorality. Usually such sins occur at night under the cover of darkness, so that sin is at least somewhat hidden. But these people do not care: they party openly in broad daylight. They misuse pleasure and daylight, both good gifts of God, in the service of sin.

They are "spots...and blemishes," the exact opposite of what Peter enjoins believers to be: without spot and blameless (2 Pet. 3:14). The last part of verse 13 is better rendered as, "Living luxuriously in their deceitfulness, they feast with you." The feast to which Peter refers is likely what is commonly called an agape (love) feast. In the apostle's day that feast often consisted of two parts: one was a supper or banquet hosted by a church member and was meant to enhance unity with other Christians; the other was the Eucharist, the celebration of the Lord's supper. Peter does not tell us explicitly of what the false teachers' deceitfulness consisted, but it is likely that those feasts had become marked by gluttony and drunkenness (1 Cor. 11:20–22), which defiled the sacrament and gave occasion for the heathen to blaspheme. Thus they were spots and blemishes, contrary to the truth of Christ, the lamb without blemish.

In addition, the false teachers have eyes full of adultery, that cannot cease from sin, and that beguile unstable souls (2 Pet. 2:14). Literally, they have "eyes full of adulteresses." Every time they see a woman, particularly an attractive woman, they are filled with carnal lust and violate the seventh commandment (Matt. 5:28). Because they look at women lustfully, they are unable to stop missing the mark (sinning). Notice that Peter does not say that they *do* not stop sinning, but that they *cannot* cease from sin. This implies the truth of total depravity, according to which man not merely *does* not cease from sin, but cannot do anything *except* sin.

Further, the false teachers beguile unstable souls. The word translated as "beguile" means to catch with bait. Peter uses this word based on his experience, since before he was called to be Jesus' disciple, he was a fisherman. The meaning is that like a fisherman who uses bait to catch fish, the false teachers seduce the unwary, luring them into all sorts of sins. They seek out those who are new to the faith and therefore somewhat ignorant, or those who are weak and indecisive in their faith. They take advantage of their uncertainty, using them to enhance their following and influence.

Another significant trait of false teachers is covetousness (2 Pet. 2:14b–16). Covetousness or covetous practices, forbidden in the tenth commandment, are avarice. While desiring something is not in itself wrong, covetousness is the desire to possess what does not rightfully belong to a person. It is also the desire always to acquire or possess more and more of what is the object of coveting—money, sex, power and influence, possessions, and other illicit cravings.

These desires arise out of the heart, the center and core of man's being from a spiritual, ethical viewpoint. As the heart is, so is the person, whether for good or for evil. This is not a one-time occurrence but is ongoing, as Peter teaches by the Greek word translated as "exercised." From this Greek word we derive our word *gymnasium*, a place in which the body is exercised and trained in the context of sports, which played a large part in Greek culture. Peter's point is that the false teachers have hearts that covetousness has trained in its crafty ways, so that they take advantage of the church in whatever ways they can.

They are therefore "cursed children." The implication of this epithet is that they are cursed by God. God's curse is the manifestation of his holy wrath against the workers of iniquity. His curse is the opposite of his blessing, which is the manifestation of his favor and pleasure. His curse, both temporally and eternally, is the revelation of God's hatred of sin, which results in his condemnation and punishment both in this life and in the life to come.

Peter reinforces his point regarding covetousness by using the example of Balaam (Num. 22–24), which is familiar to his readers, certainly to his Jewish readers. Balaam, a heathen false prophet and spiritual cousin to the New Testament false teachers, was commissioned by Balak, king of Moab, to curse Israel for a large sum of money. Balaam coveted Balak's price and attempted to call down God's curse on Israel. Despite the fact that God by a miraculous act enabled Balaam's donkey to see the angel of the Lord in the road, threatening to kill Balaam, and by the same miracle the donkey was given the power of speech by God, rebuking Balaam, he persisted in his determination to curse Israel. Despite multiple attempts to curse, in God's sovereign providence Balaam instead blessed the nation because that was God's will for Israel.

Peter's point in verses 15–16 is not all the details of the history of Balaam but his motivation of covetousness. Balaam was so blinded by his covetousness that it required a talking donkey to wake him from his madness or insanity of trying to curse those whom God had blessed. Thus he forsook the right way of God and instead went astray, following the wages of unrighteousness. He proceeded blindly on the path of eternal destruction, just as the false teachers of whom the apostle speaks.

False Teachers: Their Inevitable Doom: 2:17–22

17. These are wells without water, clouds that are carried with a tempest; to whom the mist of darkness is reserved for ever.
18. For when they speak great swelling words of vanity, they allure through the lusts of the flesh, through much wantonness, those that were clean escaped from them who live in error.
19. While they promise them liberty, they themselves are the servants of corruption: for of whom a man is overcome, of the same is he brought in bondage.
20. For if after they have escaped the pollutions of the world through the knowledge of the Lord and Saviour Jesus Christ, they are again entangled therein, the latter end is worse with them than the beginning.
21. For it had been better for them not to have known the way of righteousness, than, after they have known it, to turn from the holy commandment delivered unto them.
22. But it is happened to them according to the true proverb, The dog is turned to his own vomit again; and the sow that was washed to her wallowing in the mire.

In these verses Peter describes the end of the false teachers, mixing this with a description of the characteristics and the sins that earn them God's eternal punishment. Peter begins by calling them "wells [or springs] without water" (v. 17). Such dry wells are useless, of no benefit to those who seek refreshing water to allay their thirst. So the false teachers are of no benefit to the church. They are also clouds carried with a tempest. They are dry clouds that violently blow over the land without dropping their moisture on a thirsty land. The spiritual analogy needs no explanation.

The result is that "the mist of blackness" is reserved for them forever. Peter is intentionally redundant in this description. He speaks literally of "the blackness of darkness." He uses these double words for emphasis to describe the eternal punishment of hell that is the destination of those who lead the church astray. No one who reads these words can help but shudder at the apostle's words. Blackness of darkness is the opposite of the biblical concept of light (1 John 1:5). God's children walk in the light, as God is light; the children of evil walk in darkness. The wicked are reserved to eternal doom, that is, they may apparently sin with impunity in this life, but they are kept or guarded by God unto everlasting destruction. Their reprobation will work itself out in the way of the sin of the false teachers.

Why does Peter use such harsh words in describing the false teachers? The answer is found in verse 18: "For [because] when they speak great swelling words of vanity, they allure through the lusts of the flesh, through much wantonness, those that were clean escaped from them who live in error."

Great swelling words are immoderate, extravagant, and arrogant words. Peter does not say of what these words consist, but they cannot be the words of the gospel of salvation by God alone. Simple logic dictates that they must therefore be the lie of man's salvation of himself, the accursed doctrine of Arminianism. These are also words of vanity, that is, empty words devoid of the truth of the scriptures, words that are without purpose, words of emptiness.

The false teachers use their swelling words of vanity to allure through the lusts of the flesh and much wantonness those who have just escaped from those who live in error. Peter speaks of recent converts to the Christian faith. "Clean" escaped does not mean completely, but instead means recently or scarcely freed from their former bondage of heathenism and idol worship. Instead of helping these converts and strengthening their faith through the preaching and teaching of the gospel, the false teachers lead them astray. Although freed from their association with those who live in error, the new converts are still relatively weak in the faith and susceptible to all sorts of evils, a situation of which the false teachers take advantage.

These converts are the objects of the teachers' alluring. They entice through "the lusts of the flesh," whatever they may be—adultery, pleasure of any kind, money and wealth, possessions, fame and influence, and all that belongs to the evil world. By adding the word "wantonness," which means licentiousness, lasciviousness, or unbridled desire, Peter seems to emphasize sexual lusts. He does so by being deliberately redundant (as in verse 17, when he speaks of the blackness of darkness), speaking both of lustful desires and of sensuality. How the false teachers, guilty themselves of this lust and wantonness, could advocate the direct opposite of the gospel's teaching boggles the mind. Nevertheless, hard though this may be to understand, such is Peter's inspired teaching.

Peter continues in verse 19 to describe what makes the false teachers liable to eternal doom: "While they promise them liberty, they themselves are the servants of corruption: for of whom a man is overcome, of the same is he brought in bondage." They (false teachers) promise them (recent converts, whether Jews or Gentiles) liberty. "Liberty" is more accurately license: the freedom to do whatever one wants. The meaning cannot be liberty, because liberty is freedom from the bondage of sin through Christ, who has fulfilled the law for us (Rom. 10:4) and has enabled us to keep the law in principle as the rule of gratitude to God for his salvation. True liberty is sanctification. This is not the leadership of the false teachers. Instead, they advocate an erroneous concept of the law, according to which the fulfillment of the law means that they are free to ignore the law and live as antinomians (see Jude 4). The walk of these libertines is a walk of licentiousness that denies subjection to the law of liberty.

The apostle continues by making a sharp contrast in verse 19. While these heretics promise freedom from the law, they themselves are slaves (servants) of depravity (corruption). Peter refers to the social structure of slavery prevalent in his day, in which people were commonly slaves to their masters. "Corruption" means misery in hell and everlasting destruction. Peter uses a proverb, likely borrowed from Paul, with whose writings he was acquainted, to make his point: "Know ye not, that to whom ye yield yourselves servants to obey, his servants ye are to whom ye are to obey; whether of sin unto death, or of obedience unto righteousness?" (Rom. 6:16).

In verses 20–22 Peter describes the final destiny of the false teachers. If through the knowledge of the Lord and Savior Jesus Christ they have escaped from the pollutions of the world—and the implication is that they have—and if they have again become entangled in these pollutions, their latter end is worse than their beginning.

Peter teaches that the false teachers, to one degree or another, have escaped the pollutions or corruptions of the world. He cannot mean that they have actually and truly escaped these vices, because they again become entangled in them like a fly caught in a spider web. Nonetheless, outwardly they have rejected the pollutions of the world and have cast their lot with the church. Otherwise they could not have been in the church and could not have spread their evil doctrines within it.

The apostle goes so far as to say that they have escaped the world's defilement through "the knowledge of the Lord and Savior Jesus Christ." Peter uses Christ's full name, indicating the fullness of salvation. Without doubt the false teachers knew and understood the doctrines of salvation through the Lord and Savior Jesus Christ; they even rose to positions of leaders and teachers in the church. But their knowledge was merely formal. For a time they lived in outward and apparent sanctification, but theirs was a natural and intellectual knowledge, not the knowledge of faith. If this were not so, they could not have fallen away from the faith of the gospel.

Nor did they truly overcome the pollutions of the world after they walked for a while in the knowledge of Christ but never put their trust in him. Therefore, they were again entangled and overcome by the lusts of the flesh, wantonness, and licentiousness.

The result is that the false teachers' "end" (the term from which we derive our word *eschatology*, the doctrine of the last times) is worse than their beginning. This is the teaching of Jesus in Matthew 12:45 and in Luke 11:26, as well as in Hebrews 6:4–6. Because they have known salvation through Christ and have deliberately rejected it, their punishment is greater than that of those who have never known the truth.

In verse 21 Peter expands on his thought regarding the last clause of verse 20. He lays down a biblical principle by using the example of false teachers. If they had been legitimate teachers, they would have taught the church the way of God's righteousness, which is the life of sanctification through the redemption of Jesus Christ. They knew what "the way" was, since this was a commonly used expression in the early church. Not in a general or passing manner did they know the way, but they were thoroughly acquainted with the word of righteousness. If they had not known this way, perhaps they would have been able to plead ignorance. But this is not so. They deliberately walked in the wrong way and in heresy and attempted to turn God's people from the true way.

They also turned from "the holy commandment" given to them. The holy commandment is the gospel of Christ from the viewpoint of its content: it is the commandment to repent and believe, to turn from wickedness to holiness. But having it and understanding it, they reject it.

Therefore, it would have been better if the false teachers had not known the way and then turned their backs on the second commandment. The reason is given by Jesus in Luke 12:48: "For unto whomsoever much is given, of him shall be much required: and to whom men have committed much, of him they will ask the more." The same thought is found in Matthew 11:20–24, as well as in Hebrews 6:4–6 and 10:26–27. Peter's point is that the false teachers, knowing but rejecting the truth, will receive greater punishment than those who never hear the gospel. Having known it, it would have been better if they had never known the way of righteousness (Luke 17:1–2).

Peter concludes chapter 2 with the use of two proverbs that illustrate the falling away of the false teachers. The first is a quotation of Proverbs 26:11: "As a dog returneth to his vomit, so a fool returneth to his folly." In Peter's day dogs were not man's best friend, as they are today, but were usually wild scavengers that would eat almost everything, including their own vomit, in an effort to obtain nourishment. Like such a dog are the false teachers who return to their wicked folly.

The second proverb uses the familiar figure of a pig that wallows in the mire, becoming covered with dung and mud. It does not matter if one thoroughly washes the hog so that it is clean: the sow, given the opportunity, will return to her wallowing in the mud and once again become filthy. The warning of Jesus in Matthew 7:6 applies here: "Give not that which is holy unto the dogs, neither cast ye your pearls before swine, lest they trample them under their feet, and turn again and rend you."

CHAPTER THREE

Reminder of the Truth:
3:1–2

1. This second epistle, beloved, I now write unto you; in both which I stir up your pure minds by way of remembrance:

2. That ye may be mindful of the words which were spoken before by the holy prophets, and of the commandment of us the apostles of the Lord and Saviour:

Peter begins chapter 3 of his epistle by noting that he is writing his second epistle to the churches of Asia Minor. His implied first epistle is the letter that we call 1 Peter. He addresses the saints as "beloved," those whom he esteems and counts dear because they are one with him in the faith.

In both of his letters he intends to stir up or awaken their pure minds. The idea of "pure" is unsullied, as when one inspects a diamond in bright sunlight and finds it flawless. The reference is to the mind of the new man in Christ as it arises out of the Christian's regenerated heart. That mind is pure, or holy, and is therefore receptive to being stirred up unto remembrance. "Remembrance" implies that Peter's readers know the truth of the gospel. The apostle does not imply that they had forgotten it; there is no evidence that they had. But unlike the false teachers, they must always remember the truth and not corrupt it.

The purpose of their being stirred up unto remembrance is found in verse 2: "That [you are] mindful" of two things—the words spoken before by the holy prophets and the commandment of the apostles of the Lord. Peter wants his readers to remember the words of the prophets. The words of the prophets were the Old Testament scriptures, which comprised the majority of the Bible in Peter's day, since some of the New Testament had not yet been written. The words that the prophets spoke certainly applied to their own day, but the emphasis here falls on the words that they spoke concerning the future day of the Lord (see 1:19). This is evident from the expression "spoken before," which is to foretell or to say beforehand. The prophets are called "holy" not because they were personally perfect, but in their capacity as prophets and to distinguish them from false prophets, who abounded in the Old Testament just as false teachers abound in the New.

Peter also wants the church to remember the commandment of their apostles. He writes literally, "the commandments of your apostles, [that is], of the Lord and Saviour." "Your" is an affectionate term that indicates that those who occupied that special office belonged to the church and were beloved. The "commandment" of which Peter speaks is the command of the gospel to repent and believe. In this instance the command is the aspect of the gospel that refers to the Christian's godly walk in the world, especially with a view to resisting the doctrines and temptations of the false teachers.

There is a link between the prophets and the apostles. The prophets spoke the word of God; the apostles taught the command of the gospel. They are one and the same, both as to content and as to their effect either to save or to condemn. The reason is that both the prophets' words and the apostles' command come from "the Lord and Saviour." He is the sovereign lord and at the same time the savior, the author and finisher of our salvation.

The Ridicule of the Scoffers: 3:3–4

3. Knowing this first, that there shall come in the last days scoffers, walking after their own lusts,
4. And saying, Where is the promise of his coming? for since the fathers fell asleep, all things continue as they were from the beginning of the creation.

In walking according to the words of the prophets and the commandment of the apostles, God's people must first and above all know one thing: in the last days scoffers will come. This will occur in the last days. The reference is to the entire New Testament (Heb. 1:2; 1 Pet. 1:20). Throughout the new dispensation there will arise mockers. Although always present and active, their numbers and influence will increase as the end of time approaches.

The scoffers ridicule the teaching of scripture regarding the end times, specifically the truth of the final judgment and the events leading up to it, commonly known as the signs of the times. They do not merely deny rationally and logically the events of the last times, but they ridicule and poke fun of those who believe what scripture teaches. They regard them as narrow minded, old fashioned, and naive. Thus there is an element of deliberate nastiness in their false teachings. Peter emphasizes this by deliberately writing redundantly that in the last days there will arise scoffers, scoffing and following their own evil lusts. They intentionally reject God's revelation and instead follow their natural inclinations, desiring pleasures and lusts that are forbidden.

The arrogant scoffers deny the coming of Christ to execute God's judgment. God has commanded that all men must give account of their words and deeds. This fact the false teachers do not wish to face, since their end will be eternal damnation; this is God's promise. They deny that there is a parousia, or a second coming of the Lord.

In support of their denial of the final judgment, the false prophets assert that all things have continued unchanged since the fathers fell asleep and since the beginning of creation. That is, the final judgment has not yet taken place, although God has promised that it will. Where now is the fulfillment of that promise? What is the evidence that it will occur any time soon, or for that matter, that it will happen at all? The Old Testament fathers, beginning with Adam, died one by one. They were born, they lived their lives, and they died. Such was the natural and unremarkable course of events. Those facts are undeniable and would seem to support the mocking of the scoffers. If the fathers from the beginning of creation did not see the fulfillment of the promise of final judgment, why should it be different for the church to whom Peter writes?

This worldly and wicked philosophy is today called the theory of uniformitarianism. Uniformitarianism is the assumption that the same natural laws and processes that now operate in the universe have always operated in the same way in the universe in the past and apply everywhere. The present is the key to the past, and natural processes function at the same rate and in the same way. This is a lynchpin of the modern theory of evolutionism, which is universally accepted and taught today.

CHAPTER **THREE**

The Truth of Final Destruction: 3:5–7

5. For this they willingly are ignorant of, that by the word
    of God the heavens were of old, and the earth standing
    out of the water and in the water:
6. Whereby the world that then was, being overflowed
    with water, perished:
7. But the heavens and the earth, which are now, by the
    same word are kept in store, reserved unto fire against
    the day of judgment and perdition of ungodly men.

There is one huge problem with the theory of uniformitarianism: all things have *not* continued as they were since the fathers
died and since the beginning of creation. Such is Peter's teaching
in these verses.

He begins by asserting that the false teachers are willfully and
deliberately ignorant of the word of God. They are not merely cog-
nitively deficient, unable to understand and comprehend what the
scriptures teach. Rather, they purposely forget that by the word of
God the heavens that were of old and the earth standing out of the
water were destroyed.

Contradicting this deliberate ignoring of the truth, Peter
teaches that there is a distinction between the world that then was
(v. 6) and the heavens and earth that now are (v. 7). The defining
difference between the two worlds is the universal flood of Noah's
day (v. 6), which gives the lie to the theory of uniformitarianism.

In harmony with the Genesis account, the apostle teaches that
the basis of and predominant element of the first world—the world
that then was, the world before the flood was water. He writes
literally that by God's word the heavens existed and the earth was

71

formed through the water and by means of water (Gen. 1:9–10). Although the meaning is difficult to understand because this truth is beyond our experience, the fact that the first world had water as its basis is beyond all possibility of dispute.

Then, according to God's counsel and providence, the flood intervened. It was not a prolonged and heavy rainfall but a complete upheaval of the heavens and the earth, in which the windows of heaven were opened and the fountains of the great deep were broken up (Gen. 7:11). The entire world that then was no longer existed.

The result of that overwhelming deluge was that the principle of today's world is no longer water but fire (2 Pet. 3:7), and it will be fire that ultimately destroys the present universe. Peter teaches that the basis of this world is fire, which is taught also in the book of Revelation. Peter also teaches that those who reject scripture's instruction on this point—"ungodly men"—God has kept in store unto the day of their judgment, which will result in their utter destruction.

The commonality of Peter's teaching concerning the world of water and the world of fire is the word of God. He created by the word of his power the first world based on water (v. 5), and subsequent to the flood by the same word (v. 7) he altered it to the basis of fire. By his word, by which he accomplishes his eternal and sovereign counsel, he spoke and it took place, he commanded and it stood fast.

The truth of the word of God is the destruction of the theory of uniformitarianism and the consequent theory of evolutionism. Everything that lived in the first world was destroyed by water to make room for a world of fire. Everything that lives in the present world will be destroyed to make room for the new heavens and earth. But for uniformitarianism and evolutionism there is no scheme or room, according to the word of God. The same God who spoke by water as creator will speak as judge by fire. Despite the mocking of the scoffers, the coming of the Lord is sure.

The Lord's Timeless Promise: 3:8-9

8. But, beloved, be not ignorant of this one thing, that one day is with the Lord as a thousand years, and a thousand years as one day.
9. The Lord is not slack concerning his promise, as some men count slackness; but is longsuffering to us-ward, not willing that any should perish, but that all should come to repentance.

Peter's first answer to the uniformitarian deniers of Christ's coming for judgment was that there is an essential difference between the first world and the second world, the division being the flood. The basis of the first was water, while the basis of the second is fire. Therefore, the scoffers' premise is false.

His second answer to the scoffers is found in these verses and has to do with the correct understanding of time and eternity. Thus the apostle admonishes his beloved fellow Christians not to forget what he is about to tell them.

Time, like everything else in the present world, is a creature of God. It began with creation and will end at the parousia (Rev. 10:6). As far as man is concerned, time governs his entire existence from the cradle to the grave; all of his counting, including his reckoning of slackness, is based on time; he is a creature of time.

But with God this is not so. God is the eternal one who is not bound or governed by time, for he is above time. Instead, he uses time and all that occurs within it to realize his eternal counsel, his intention to glorify himself through the salvation of his people in Christ. In a word, for God, the absolute and eternal one, time is relative.

This is why Peter can assert that with the Lord a day is like a thousand years, and a thousand years as one day. In so doing, he quotes Psalm 90:4: "For a thousand years in thy sight are but as yesterday when it is past, and as a watch in the night." The movement of time does not matter to God. To man it does, because governed by time as he is, and having only a limited span of existence, man is impatient. He cannot wait for what he thinks should happen when it should happen. In this way Peter refutes the challenge of the scoffers that Christ will not come in judgment. God does not reckon time as do the mockers, who think that if God has not yet fulfilled his promise of final judgment, he never will.

Peter reinforces his point by writing that God is not slack or slow concerning his promise. The promise of which he speaks is the coming of the Lord through Christ, who is always centrally the content of the promise throughout history. God's promise has not yet completely come, but it is coming with all speed. God does not slacken or hurry the fulfillment of his counsel, but he realizes it as soon as possible. He thus directly contradicts the mockers.

Peter teaches instead that God is longsuffering to us-ward, not willing that any should perish, but that all should come to repentance. God, as it were, is slow, not in a hurry to realize his promise.

Arminians use this verse to support their doctrine of universal salvation based on man's free will. They teach that God desires to save all men, but that their salvation depends on man's acceptance or rejection of God's free offer of grace, which is necessary to believe. They misuse Peter's statement that God is not willing that all should perish, but that all should come to repentance, as a proof text for their doctrine of universal salvation.

Peter's teaching could not be farther from this heresy. His key word is "longsuffering" (v. 9). This word carries in it the idea of patience or an enduring long. The importance of the term is that the object of God's longsuffering is his elect people, in contrast to the biblical word *forbearance*, which has the wicked as its object.

Peter speaks of God's longsuffering in the context of the coming of Christ, which is the subject at hand. If his longsuffering means that God delays his coming until all have believed, then the parousia will never come. This is ridiculously impossible, since all have not and will not believe.

Rather, Peter teaches that God suffers long and is patient regarding the parousia in order that in history his people can be saved. They must be born, they must hear the gospel, they must believe, and they must be saved. Christ's coming must not be rushed and must not be premature. According to his sovereign counsel, God wills that all his people must come to repentance and that the promise of his coming cannot be fulfilled until not one is lost. Then will come the end.

The Coming of the End: 3:10–13

10. But the day of the Lord will come as a thief in the night; in the which the heavens shall pass away with a great noise, and the elements shall melt with fervent heat, the earth also and the works that are therein shall be burned up.

11. Seeing then that all these things shall be dissolved, what manner of persons ought ye to be in all holy conversation and godliness,

12. Looking for and hasting unto the coming of the day of God, wherein the heavens being on fire shall be dissolved, and the elements shall melt with fervent heat?

13. Nevertheless we, according to his promise, look for new
heavens and a new earth, wherein dwelleth righteousness.

In these verses Peter continues the subject of the coming of the
Lord by describing his second advent. Peter begins by stating that
the day of the Lord will come as a thief in the night. The phrase "in
the night" should probably not be included in the text, but its omis-
sion does not essentially change the meaning: the day of the Lord
will come like a thief, that is, unexpectedly and without warning.
From his Greek word we derive the English word *kleptomaniac*,
one who surreptitiously steals.

Scripture in many places reveals the signs of Christ's second
coming, detailing what must happen to bring about his parousia
and for what the church must watch as the end draws near. But it
does so only in general terms, at the same time teaching that we
may not attempt to determine the exact time and circumstances
of his advent, for even Christ does not know the exact time, but
only the Father. In this context Peter teaches that in the final
analysis the day of the Lord will come like a thief. There is an element of suddenness and unexpectedness regarding the finality of
the end of all things. Despite the signs of the times, the parousia
will sneak up on mankind; thus the signs and the exact time are
reconciled.

In contradiction of the denial of Christ's coming, Peter's
description of the end of all things is threefold: the heavens will
pass away with a great noise; the elements will melt with fervent
heat; and the earth and its contents will be burned up. These events
must be understood in the context of 3:7, which teaches that the
principle of the present world is not water but fire.

First, the heavens will pass away with a great noise. In speaking of a great noise, Peter uses a word that appears only here in

scripture. It means a great roar. Of what this consists we cannot be certain. But one cannot help but think of the current secular theory of the origin of the universe, called the "Big Bang Theory." According to it, the universe came into being by means of a cosmic cataclysm, the source of which cannot be determined. Perhaps this theory, reinterpreted in the light of scripture, has some validity. God spoke his creative word and instantly (with a great bang?) the heavens came into being. At the end of time there will be a great roar—not the noise of creation, but the roar of utter and final destruction. Could this be the reverse of a possible "Big Bang" of creation? Whether or not this is true, the event is fearfully indescribable and inconceivable.

Second, the elements will melt with fervent heat. There is difference of opinion as to the meaning of "elements." Some think that it refers to earth, water, and air. Others think that the word means the celestial bodies—sun, moon, and stars. However, in harmony with the original word, it is better to understand elements as the first principles of the material universe. Elements are that from which all things derive their existence, the material causes of the universe. The very building blocks—the molecules and atoms—of all things will melt and dissolve, so that the entire universe will burn and crash into destruction. It will not be annihilated, for out of its ruins God will form the new heavens and earth. But the present universe will be no more.

Third, the earth and the works in it will be burned up. So that there can be no misunderstanding, Peter is careful to include the earth in the final destruction. Not only the earth itself, but also the works that are in it will be demolished. The reference is not to the deeds or actions of men, which cannot be destroyed, but to the works of man in the sense of the contents of the earth. All that man has built and developed over the course of the entire history of the earth—his towering skyscrapers, his technology, his military might, and all of his accomplishments and achievements—will be dissolved and will go out of existence. Mighty man's works will meet the almighty counsel and power of God, and the result will be the complete destruction of man's works.

In verses 11 and 12 Peter applies practically what he has just written. He does so by a rhetorical question: seeing that all of these destructive events will inevitably occur, what kind of people ought you to be?

He begins by saying "seeing then" or "consequently," thus drawing a conclusion from his teaching in the preceding verses. After speaking of the fact that the entire universe will be dissolved in the day of the Lord, the apostle gives an implied admonition in the form of a question: what manner of people ought you to be?

Peter answers his question by saying, "in all holy conversation and godliness." "Conversation" does not mean talking, as it does in our common usage, but is used in scripture to mean one's manner of life or behavior. Synonyms are *walk* or *conduct*. The walk of God's people should be one of godliness, that is, an attitude of reverence and of obedience toward God.

Such a walk is not optional for Christians. This is clear from the word "ought" that Peter uses. His point is that our walk of life *must* be one of godliness and obedience to God's will. In light of the impending destruction of all things, Peter challenges his readers to live as if the coming of the Lord can happen at any time. Thus they should live as those whose final salvation is near, and they should behave accordingly.

Peter further describes Christians as those who look for and haste to the coming of the day of the Lord (v. 12). To look for is to expect or to wait for something not in fear but in hope, for the coming of the Lord means the believers' salvation—the return of Christ to raise the dead, to judge all men and angels, and to establish the eternal kingdom of glory, of which they are heirs by grace.

Those who walk in godliness are also described as those who hasten the coming of the day of God. Their walking and their hastening are connected, but not in the sense that by their actions the time of the day of God is actually advanced. This cannot be because the time of the end is forever fixed in his counsel. Yet there is a sense in which God's people, at least from their viewpoint, speed his coming. They do this by their prayers, by the preaching of the gospel (Matt. 24:14), by the repentance of God's elect (Acts 3:19–21), and by living holy and godly lives. Always their prayer is, "Come, Lord Jesus. Come quickly!"

In the last part of verse 12, Peter re-emphasizes what he taught in verse 11 regarding the dissolution of all things; this requires no further explanation. He wants to be sure that the church understands the nature and scope of the end of all things: the day of God will bring about the destruction of the heavens by fire, and the elements will melt with intense heat, the like of which has never happened.

"Nevertheless", according to God's promise that cannot fail, "we...look for new heavens and a new earth, wherein dwelleth righteousness (2 Pet 3:13; Rev. 21:1). Out of the wreckage of the present universe, God will recreate a new heavens and a new earth.

This creation will be new because it will be characterized by the perfection of God himself and of Christ. Also the citizens of the new kingdom, the angels and the redeemed, will be characterized by the righteousness of God in Christ, both in the legal, juridical sense and in the spiritual, ethical sense. They will be fully and perfectly righteous. In the new creation there will be no more sin, evil, and darkness, but only perfection, goodness, and light.

The perfection of the new creation will be eternal for all God's people. This is the significance of the dwelling of righteousness in the new creation. Righteousness will live and abide in it. Also in the present creation there is righteousness, for God created it perfect. But righteousness did not dwell in it permanently, because it did not remain. It could be and was lost. But in the new creation it cannot be lost, because Christ's finished righteousness is its ground and foundation, and this righteousness can never fail.

Admonition to be Diligent: 3:14–15a

14. Wherefore, beloved, seeing that ye look for such things, be diligent that ye may be found of him in peace, without spot, and blameless.
15a. And account that the longsuffering of our Lord is salvation.

"Wherefore" draws a conclusion from what Peter has just written and at the same time introduces the next admonition. Because they eagerly anticipate the coming of the Lord, believers must behave in a certain way. Undoubtedly Peter expects their compliance with his admonition, because he addresses them as "beloved," that is, as his dear friends whom he loves and who love him because they share a common faith.

Peter wants his readers to do two things: be diligent to be found in peace without spot or blemish and account that the longsuffering of the Lord is salvation. He qualifies his double admonition by the phrase "seeing that ye look for such things" (v. 14).

By "such things" the apostle refers to the preceding context, including the day of the Lord, the destruction of the present world, and the renewal of all things. When he writes "looking for," he has in mind the idea of hope. Peter has rightly been called the apostle of hope, and although he does not use the word, hope is the concept of which he writes here.

Hope concerns, first, the future (Rom. 8:24–25). Second, hope implies a longing for a future good (essentially, full salvation, but never for anything unfavorable or undesirable). Third, unlike our use of the term, which implies uncertainty, hope is the absolute certainty that the object of hope will come to pass.

Based on this hope, God's people must be found to be without spot and blameless. This leaves no room for an evil walk of life. They must put forth every effort to be spotless, that is, irreproachable and unsullied by the wicked world and its sin. They must also be unblemished, those who cannot be reproached or censured for their conduct. Because of their hope and its object, they must be spotless and blameless. Because we cannot inherit the new creation unless we dwell in righteousness, it follows that our hope of the future means that we must be diligent to live in sanctification, being without imperfection.

Christians, being spotless and blameless, must also be found in peace. Peace is harmony, first with God and his will and commandments, and second with our fellow beloved brethren in the faith. Peace is the sphere in which God's people are spotless and blameless.

In the second part of his admonition to the church, Peter says that believers must "account that the longsuffering of our Lord is salvation" (2 Pet. 3:15). The church was correctly and in a good sense somewhat impatient for the coming of the Lord ("hasting unto," v. 12). Peter has already instructed the church that God is not slack concerning his promise (v. 9), and now he reiterates that thought in terms of longsuffering. God's apparent postponement or delay of his coming must be attributed to his longsuffering, which is his desire to save his elect in the way of and by means of their suffering as they live in the wicked world. This longsuffering, the church must remember, is salvation. Despite their being persecuted, the church must reckon that he is the God of their salvation, who saves them speedily according to his counsel and promise.

The Wisdom of Paul:
3:15b–16

15b. Even as our beloved brother Paul also according to the wisdom given unto him hath written unto you;

16. As also in all his epistles, speaking in them of these things; in which are some things hard to be understood, which they that are unlearned and unstable wrest, as they do also the other scriptures, unto their own destruction.

In these verses Peter confirms what he has just written about the coming of the Lord by appealing to the writings of Paul, his fellow apostle. The connection is established in verse 15 by "even as," indicating agreement between Peter and Paul.

Moreover, Peter calls Paul his beloved brother. The only known instance in which they tangled was when Paul rebuked Peter for his hypocrisy in not eating with the Gentiles when the Jews were present (Gal. 2:11–14), and this issue was quickly resolved. Other than that, their relationship was apparently harmonious. Paul mentions Peter several times in 1 Corinthians (1:12; 3:22; 9:5; 15:5). Paul visited Peter for fifteen days (Gal. 1:18), and they met at the Jerusalem council (Acts 15:6–21). This association is important because it confirms that Paul taught the same gospel as did Peter.

Peter goes on to say that Paul has written the same things to the same saints of Asia Minor ("you"). Paul wrote a total of thirteen canonical books to the churches, and some of them the churches of Asia Minor obviously possessed, although it is uncertain which of these they had received at this time. Paul writes, says Peter, "according to the wisdom given to him," a clear reference to the inspiration of scripture (2 Pet. 4:15). The Holy Spirit gave him wisdom, so that he had the necessary knowledge and skill to impart the Christian faith to God's people.

Whatever the facts may be, the wisdom given to Paul concerns "these things" (v. 16). The reference is not exclusively to the longsuffering of God (v. 15), although this is surely included. Rather, Peter has in mind the coming of the Lord, together with all its aspects, including those he has specified. More narrowly, Peter refers to his admonition to the church to live and walk in sanctification with a view to the coming of the Lord and his longsuffering.

In Paul's writings are "some things hard to be understood," says Peter (v. 16). Why he makes this personal comment about Paul's writings, as he surely does, is difficult if not impossible to know. Does Peter mean to imply that Paul should simplify and clarify his writings so that the church can more easily understand that he writes concerning "these things"? Or does he merely state a fact? If so, why does he even make this statement? Could the implication be that at the time of Peter's epistle some of Paul's writings are unclear, but that their meaning will become clearer in the future through his further writings, so that the church will develop in the truth of the end times? The answer is well-nigh impossible to ascertain. It is not amiss in this connection to remark that there are also some things in Peter's writings that are hard to understand.

These things that are hard to understand the unlearned and unstable wrest. Peter describes them as unlearned. Undoubtedly referring to the false teachers of his day, Peter has in mind those

KNOWING GOD IN THE LAST DAYS

who present themselves as teachers but are ignorant of the truth of scripture. Therefore, they are unstable in their teachings and are tossed about by every wind of doctrine (Eph. 4:14).

This ignorance and instability extend beyond Paul's difficult writings to "other scriptures." These are the Old Testament scriptures, which throughout speak of the coming of the Lord, not only of his first coming in the advent of Christ, but also of his second and final coming at the end of time.

These unlearned and unstable wrest the truth. Although they are unlearned and unstable, there is an element of deliberateness in their heresies. They twist—literally torture— both the Old Testament writings and Paul's teachings. The result is their utter and complete destruction in the eternal misery of hell.

Concluding Admonition: 3:17–18

17. Ye therefore, beloved, seeing ye know these things before, beware lest ye also, being led away with the error of the wicked, fall from your own stedfastness.
18. But grow in grace, and in the knowledge of our Lord and Saviour Jesus Christ. To him be glory both now and for ever. Amen.

Beware! This is the first of Peter's two concluding admonitions. Addressing the church as "beloved," he draws ("therefore") a conclusion from the previous verses, sharply contrasting the distorters of scripture with the truth he has taught. All of the truths concerning the coming of the Lord the believers already knew, according to Peter. From the words "know before" we derive the English word *prognosis*, which is self-explanatory. Therefore, God's people must always be on guard, lest the error of the wicked false teachers lead them astray and they fall from their own steadfastness in the faith.

The key to the prevention of this falling is the spiritual knowledge of our Lord and Savior Jesus Christ, which knowledge is mentioned twice in these two verses. When the church knows the truth, specifically regarding the coming of Christ, it cannot be led astray by the wicked and cannot fall from its steadfastness in adhering to the truth.

This is possible only by growing in grace (v. 18). To grow in grace is to increase in all the virtues of grace—faith, hope, love, assurance of our calling and justification, the forgiveness of our sins, and our walk in sanctification. Because we are redeemed by our Lord and Savior Jesus Christ, all of God's people grow in his knowledge and grace. Then in the words of the chain of chapter 1, we add to our faith virtue, to virtue knowledge, to knowledge temperance, to temperance patience, to patience godliness, to godliness brotherly kindness, and to brotherly kindness charity.

Peter ends his letter to the churches by ascribing glory and praise to God. Never must there be anything of man in his own salvation. It is only the work of our Lord and Savior Jesus Christ. All is the work of God alone according to his counsel and by means of his sovereign power. This is true "both now and forever," literally "into the day of the ages," into the eternal day of the new creation (v. 18).

Peter appropriately concludes his letter to the churches with "Amen," that is, "It will certainly be." We can only echo his sentiment: Amen!

www.ingramcontent.com/pod-product-compliance
Lightning Source LLC
Chambersburg PA
CBHW060751100426
42813CB00004B/773